ALL THE GREAT BOOKS
(abridged)

ALL THE GREAT BOOKS
(abridged)

by Reed Martin and Austin Tichenor

Additional material by Matthew Croke and Michael Faulkner

JW

JOSEF WEINBERGER PLAYS

LONDON

ALL THE GREAT BOOKS (ABRIDGED)
First published in 2008
by Josef Weinberger Ltd
12-14 Mortimer Street, London, W1T 3JJ
www.josef-weinberger.com   general.info@jwmail.co.uk

UK edition Copyright © 2008 by Reed Martin and Austin Tichenor
Copyright © 2002 by Reed Martin and Austin Tichenor

The authors asserts their moral right to be identified as the authors of the work.

ISBN 978 085676 293 2

This play is protected by Copyright. According to Copyright Law, no public performance or reading of a protected play or part of that play may be given without prior authorisation from Josef Weinberger Plays, as agent for the Copyright Owners.

From time to time it is necessary to restrict or even withdraw the rights of certain plays. **It is therefore essential to check with us before making a commitment to produce a play.**

NO PERFORMANCE MAY BE GIVEN WITHOUT A LICENCE

AMATEUR PRODUCTIONS
Royalties are due at least thirty days prior to the first performance. A royalty quotation will be issued upon receipt of the following details:

Name of Licensee
Play Title
Place of Performance
Dates and Number of Performances
Audience Capacity
Ticket Prices

PROFESSIONAL PRODUCTIONS
All enquiries regarding professional English Language performance rights outside North America should be addressed to Josef Weinberger Plays at the address above. Enquiries for stock and amateur performance rights in North America should be addressed to Broadway Play Publishing Inc, 56 E 81st Street, New York, NY 10028.

OVERSEAS PRODUCTIONS
Applications for productions overseas (other than North America) should be addressed to our local authorised agents. Further details are listed in our catalogue of plays, published every two years, or available from Josef Weinberger Plays at the address above.

CONDITIONS OF SALE
This book is sold subject to the condition that it shall not by way of trade or otherwise be resold, hired out, circulated or distributed without prior consent of the Publisher. **Reproduction of the text either in whole or part and by any means is strictly forbidden.**

Printed by Commercial Colour Press plc, Hainault, Essex, England

IMPORTANT NOTE:

The name "Reduced Shakespeare Company" ® is a Registered Trademark, and its use in any way whatsoever to publicise, promote, or advertise any performance of this script is EXPRESSLY PROHIBITED.

Likewise, any use of the name "Reduced Shakespeare Company" ® within the actual live performance of this script is also EXPRESSLY PROHIBITED.

The play must be billed as follows:

ALL THE GREAT BOOKS (abridged)

By

REED MARTIN & AUSTIN TICHENOR
Additional Material by Matthew Croke and Michael Faulkner

ABOUT THE AUTHORS

Reed Martin

Reed is a Managing Partner of the Reduced Shakespeare Company, which he joined in 1989. He co-created and performed in the original stage productions of **The Complete History of America (abridged)**, **The Bible: The Complete Word of God (abridged)**, **Western Civilization: The Complete Musical (abridged), Completely Hollywood (abridged),** and **All The Great Books (abridged)** – and contributed additional material to **The Complete Works of William Shakespeare (abridged)**.

Reed has written for the BBC, National Public Radio, Britain's Channel Four, RTE Ireland, Public Radio International, the Washington Post, and Vogue Magazine. With Austin Tichenor he wrote the comic memoir **The Greatest Story Ever Sold**, as well as the comic reference book **Reduced Shakespeare** which is published by Hyperion.

He has been seen on all the major television networks, and has performed in forty-six states and eleven foreign countries.

Prior to joining the Reduced Shakespeare Company, Reed spent two years as a clown and assistant ringmaster with Ringling Brothers' Barnum & Bailey Circus.

Reed has a BA in Theatre/Political Science from the University of California at Berkeley and an MFA in Acting from the University of California at San Diego. He is also a graduate of both Ringling Brothers' Barnum & Bailey Clown College and the Bill Kinnamon School of Professional Baseball Umpire Training. He lives in Northern California with his wife and two sons.

Austin Tichenor

Austin is a Managing Partner of the Reduced Shakespeare Company, which he joined in 1992. He co-created and performed in the original stage productions of **Completely Hollywood (abridged), All The Great Books (abridged), Western Civilization: The Complete Musical (abridged), The Bible: The Complete Word of God (abridged),** and **The Complete History of America (abridged)**. He also starred in the PBS film version of **The Complete Works of William Shakespeare (abridged)**.

Prior to joining the RSC, Austin was Associate Producing Director of the American Stage Festival in Milford, NH, where he created "Early Stages", ASF's New Play Series, served as Literary Manager/Dramaturg, wrote stage adaptations of *A Christmas Carol* and *Frankenstein*, and directed several productions a season. He also developed ASF's Young Company, for which he wrote over twenty original plays and musicals for young audiences.

With his partner Dee Ryan, Austin wrote and developed the animated project **Fowl Play** for Disney, as well as the screenplays **Birds of a Feather** and **All The Other Reindeer**. With Reed Martin, he wrote the comic memoir **The Greatest Story Ever Sold**, as well as **Reduced Shakespeare** which is published by Hyperion. And he's guest starred on many hours of episodic television, including recurring roles on **Everwood, 24, Alias, The Practice, Mister Sterling, Ally McBeal,** and **Felicity,** in addition to several movies and national commercials.

Austin has a BA in History and Dramatic Art from UC Berkeley and an MFA in Directing from Boston University. He's a member of the Dramatists Guild and an alumnus of the BMI Musical Theatre Workshop. He lives in Los Angeles with his wife and two children.

Special Thanks

For their contributions to the development of the script, the Authors wish to thank Jane Martin, Dee Ryan, Megan Loughney, Don Martin, Lisa Croke, Viola Voris, Rachel Hamilton, Russell Lees, Leila and Robert Gordon, Ezra Weiss and Peter & Aliza Murrieta of LA's Bang Improv Studio, Charles Towers and Merrimack Repertory Theatre, Ed Stern and Cincinnati Playhouse in the Park, Geoff Alm, Steve Smith, Guillermo Gonzalez, Kent Thompson & Alan Harrison and Alabama Shakespeare Festival, Kea Watson, Andrea Atkins, and the audiences who came and laughed (or didn't) at the early workshops. Very special thanks to Matt and Mike, who made this thing come alive in rehearsal by finding the funny (and often adding it).

FOR WHAT IT'S WORTH:

Although within the published script we use the name "Matt" for the student teacher character and "Professor Tichenor" for the drama teacher, the actors playing these roles in your production should be referred to by their actual first and last names. The third character is always simply referred to as "Coach". You can cast an actor with no actual first and last names if you so choose.

There are a number of topical references in the script. The humour and relevance of some of these will fade over time, so we encourage each production to keep these references as up-to-date as possible. This is not to say that scenes should be rewritten (which is, in fact, strictly prohibited) but rather we are giving you permission to change a punchline or reference from "Kato Kaelin" to "Paris Hilton", or from "Lyndon Johnson" to "George W Bush".

The production elements described in the script are from the original Reduced Shakespeare Company production. Consequently the scenery, props and costumes were all reduced in both quality and number. We'd encourage you to do the same. The conceit is not only that we are reducing *All The Great Books*, but everything within the production as well. There are only three actors and the setting is a high school theatre. In theory, all the props and costumes in the show are being borrowed from the storage room of the high school drama department. It should look like you are flying by the seat of your pants and not like you've had months to come up with a fabulous design for the show. It's more charming if the whole thing looks like it's being made up on the spot.

In our experience, the script works best when it is performed simply and seriously. That is to say, the script is funny so play it straight. Keep the show moving. For God's sake, don't linger. Many of the punchlines are meant to be throwaways. And for those of you who think the whole script should be thrown away, we can only say we tried that and it didn't work nearly as well.

ALL THE GREAT BOOKS (ABRIDGED) was originally produced and performed by the Reduced Shakespeare Company. The first public performance was at bang. Improv Studio in Hollywood, CA on 24 January 2002 with the following cast:

Coach – Reed Martin
Professor – Austin Tichenor
Student Teacher – Michael Faulkner

The show was performed at Merrimack Repertory Theatre in Lowell, MA in March 2002, at Cincinnati Playhouse in the Park in July 2002, and at Alabama Shakespeare Festival in August 2002 with the following cast:

Coach – Reed Martin
Professor – Michael Faulkner
Student Teacher – Matthew Croke

The show then opened at the Kennedy Center in Washington, DC on 12 June 2003 with the following cast:

Coach – Reed Martin
Professor – Austin Tichenor
Student Teacher – Matthew Croke

ALL THE GREAT BOOKS (ABRIDGED) was first performed in the United Kingdom at the Pleasance One Theatre, Edinburgh on 8 August 2003 prior to a national tour, with the following cast:

Coach – Reed Martin
Professor – Austin Tichenor
Student Teacher – Matthew Croke

Directors	Reed Martin and Austin Tichenor
General Manager	Megan Loughney
Technical Director	Kea Watson
Fight Director	Geoffrey Alm
Creative Consultant	Steve Smith
Scenic Design	Robertson Wellen
Props	Erika Lilienthal, Shannon Rae Lutz, Jenni Schwaner, Kea Watson
Costumes	Erika Lilienthal, Frances Nelson McSherry, Jenni Schwaner, Allison Stubbs
Dickensian Organ Riffs	Charlie Christmas
Additional Voice	Jane Martin

ALL THE GREAT BOOKS (ABRIDGED)

ACT ONE

The scene is a high school auditorium. An American flag hangs from its pole stage right. A white drawing board stands stage left; on it, "All The Great Books" is written in black marker. The scenery is a backdrop painted as a library: floor-to-ceiling shelves covered with Great Books. Framed portraits and busts of Great Authors decorate the shelves. There are two doors, right and left of upstage centre, a real bookshelf between the two doorways, and a chair. The pre-show music finishes with a very loud song, in the midst of which we hear a school bell ring, followed by a coach's whistle. COACH *enters from the back of the house. He wears long athletic shorts, tall tube socks, baseball cap, a whistle, a stopwatch and carries a bag full of various sports balls.*

COACH (*talking over the loud music*) Alright everybody, settle down. Stop your private conversations. Put your personal items away. Turn off the radio!

(*The music stops.*)

Thank you. I'd like to welcome you to class, my name is . . . (*writes on the board*) . . . Coach. Now we all know why we're here. This is a repeat course for those of you who didn't pass your Western Literature requirement last term. The Parent Teacher Association and Principal Wilcox require that you pass this course in order to graduate. Graduation is in one hour and forty-five minutes. (*He starts his stopwatch.*) Before we go any further, I've been asked to make a few announcements. (*He pulls a piece of paper out of his cap and reads.*) There is a school basketball game tonight in the gymnasium at 7.30 against the opponents. University entrance exams are scheduled for Saturday morning at 9.00 AM. (*Looks over the audience.*) Probably doesn't apply to anyone here. Today's hot lunch is Sloppy Joes and peach cobbler. The vegetable is ketchup. And now ladies and gentlemen, without further ado, all the great books.

ACT ONE

Eighty-nine books. (*Thirty-six books are thrown on from the wings. We know that the text of the script mentions eighty-six books, but no one is going to count them. Three of the books have actual pages. The rest have the pages removed and replaced with foam. This makes them less likely to fall apart when they get thrown around. NB: They've been thrown by the other two actors.*)

(PROFESSOR *runs on. He wears glasses, a pink sweater vest, bow tie, and slacks.*)

PROFESSOR How was it?

COACH A little bit much I thought.

PROFESSOR The great books need a great entrance. I thought it was very theatrical.

COACH Yes, well, you would. I'm sure all of you know Mr Tichenor, our drama teacher.

PROFESSOR (*with a Shakespearean flourish*) I am but a humble player . . .

COACH (*trying to go on*) Yes . . .

PROFESSOR . . . who struts and frets his hour upon the stage and is heard no more.

COACH That would be a great idea. Now, you may also be aware that our regular literature teacher was tragically trampled to death at a JK Rowling book signing. Since no one else was available on such short notice to teach the course, we eagerly volunteered.

PROFESSOR We leapt at the chance.

COACH Yes, we were thrilled.

PROFESSOR Now we won't be asking anyone to pledge allegiance to the American flag because the entire class seems to be comprised of foreign exchange students. In fact, are there any Americans here at all? (*Pretend that someone raises his or her hand even if nobody does.*) There are? Okay, then we'll speak slowly.

(MATT *runs on, carrying a book. He wears cargo pants, T-shirt covered by an unbuttoned Hawaiian shirt, and backwards baseball cap.*)

MATT Sorry! Sorry I'm late! Sorry students, sorry I'm late.

COACH You should be. I'm sure many of you know our very late student teacher, Matt.

MATT (*to audience*) Woo!

COACH Where were you?

MATT (*revealing the book*) Reading *Lord of the Rings*, baby! Man, can you believe they made a book out of the movie?

COACH/PROFESSOR Matt!

MATT I just wanna say that you students are very lucky. When I went to school here, I didn't have great teachers like Coach or Mr Tichenor.

PROFESSOR Matthew, please. Mr Tichenor is my father. Call me Professor.

COACH (*to* MATT, *re: the books*) Straighten these up.

(MATT *exits to get a large push broom. He quickly reenters and begins to sweep all the books into a pile downstage.*)

So, students. What do we mean by "The Great Books"? Anyone? No? Well, I'm not surprised. And this is exactly why we're holding class in the school theatre. It's the

only room on campus large enough to
accommodate this many remedial students.

PROFESSOR   And being in the school theatre will allow us to
dramatize all the great books using my
extensive collection of props and costumes, as
well as – (*He gestures to the backdrop.*) The
backdrop from my controversial production of
My Fair Lady.

COACH   Now this is an awful lot of material to cover in
a very short period of time because, as you can
see, all the great books are here. *Ulysses. The
Iliad. The Odyssey. Remembrance of Things
Past. Moby Dick. Don Quixote.* Charles
Dickens. And of course . . .

(MATT *drops one huge book – approximately
2' X 1' X 6" in size – on the floor. BANG! [It
was preset on the bookshelf up-centre.] All
three bounce slightly from the vibration.*)

. . . *War and Peace.*

PROFESSOR   If you could all take a look at your syllabus,
which is in the handout you received on your
way in, you'll notice we won't be covering
every great book.

COACH   No, only the eighty-six *greatest* books.

(*The three teachers have pulled out syllabi
and refer to them.*)

MATT   Wait a second, wait a second. *Lord of the
Rings* isn't on here.

COACH   Nope. Nor is *The Communist Manifesto*.

PROFESSOR   That's right. No fantasy. But there's still
plenty of material on here familiar to everyone.
In fact, could I see by a show of hands, how
many of you have ever read anything by Mister
Charles Dickens? Charles Dickens, anyone?

COACH/MATT	Great!

(They run off.)

PROFESSOR Now, our goal is to make these great works of literature come alive for you. And as your drama teacher, and the proud holder of a GNVQ in theatre – *(Picking a book from the floor.)* – from *(Insert name of sub-par local technical or community college here; if the audience applauds or cheers this,* PROFESSOR *can say "I see some of you have been accepted there this fall.")*, the only way I know to make literature come alive is through the magic of theatre! And that's why I love Charles Dickens. *(Flipping through the pages.)* Each of his novels is filled with exaggerated characterizations, action-packed plots, and cliffhanger endings. And so to give you a taste of the anticipation and drama experienced by the 19th century reader, we are proud to present to you Charles Dickens' continuing soap opera –

(Soap opera music begins.)

Great Expectorations. Brought to you by Tidy Kid. Four out of five indentured child laborers prefer Tidy Kid over the second leading brand. Tidy Kid. It beats a beating. And now, Episode Seventeen of *Great Expectorations: A Sale of Two Titties.* Charles Darnay, trapped in prison, is being interrogated by the evil Madame Defarge.

(COACH *and* MATT *enter as their characters are introduced.* COACH *wears handcuffs and kneels centre.* MATT *wears a skirt and wig.* PROFESSOR *exits.)*

MATT (*as* MADAME DEFARGE) It is the best of times.

COACH (*as* DARNAY) It is the worst of times.

MATT/DEFARGE You will not live to see another day, Monsieur Darnay. You French Aristocrats have destroyed Albert Square (*or other fictional soap opera locale*)! But we, the Bold and the Beautiful are now the Young and the Restless! Our day has come!

COACH/DARNAY You must recant your lies so that I can return to my loving wife Lucie Manette and our four little ones.

MATT/DEFARGE Ha! There are no longer four. We have already executed Jean-Renault.

COACH/DARNAY You shot JR?

MATT/DEFARGE *Oui!*

(*They exit. The* PROFESSOR *enters.*)

PROFESSOR Meanwhile, on the other side of the English Channel in London, we see Oliver Twist.

(MATT *enters dressed as* OLIVER TWIST.)

MATT/OLIVER Come on, baby, let's do the –

PROFESSOR (*as* BOSS) Stop dancing, Oliver! Get back to work!

(PROFESSOR *exits.* MATT *cleans the floor with a rag and bottle of cleanser.*)

MATT/OLIVER It's a hard knock life. Lucky for me, I'm using Tidy Kid. (*He turns the bottle upside down, indicating that it's empty.*) Please, sir, may I have some more?

(COACH *enters as* SCROOGE.)

COACH/SCROOGE   Bah, humbug.

MATT/OLIVER   Then may I leave early, sir? It's Christmas Eve.

COACH/SCROOGE   I suppose you'll want Christmas Day off, as well.

MATT/OLIVER   If it's convenient.

COACH/SCROOGE   It's not convenient.

MATT/OLIVER   If you don't give me the time off, I'll be forced to reveal your dark secret to all of the Desperate Housewives!

(Organ sting.)

COACH/SCROOGE   Which dark secret?

(Sting.)

MATT/OLIVER   That you and Jacob Marley were more than just business partners!

(We hear the famous baseball game organ chords, exhorting the crowd to yell, "Do do do do-do". COACH and MATT both do a pelvic thrust in time to the music then exit. The PROFESSOR enters, and more soap opera music plays through his next speech.)

PROFESSOR   Will Charles Darnay escape from prison? Will Oliver star in a Broadway musical? Will Scrooge and Marley get married in San Francisco? The answer to these and other questions will be found next week in Episode Eighteen of *Great Expectorations*, when we see David Copperfield date a German supermodel and make the Statue of Liberty disappear.

(Blackout as the music swells. The lights come up as the music goes out and COACH and MATT enter.)

MATT	That was great. In that last section we covered – (*picks up four books*) Dickens, Dickens, Dickens, Dickens, and –
	(PROFESSOR *tosses his Dickens book to* MATT.)
	Dickens! Five books down, eighty-one more to go.
	(MATT *carries the books upstage and places them on the bookshelf.*)
PROFESSOR	Very good. I'd like to move on now to the Great Poets.
COACH	(*starting to go*) Great.
MATT	Oh, I can help with this! (*Recites.*) "I will not do it in a boat. I will not do it with a goat . . ."
COACH/ PROFESSOR	Matt!
PROFESSOR	Matthew, I know Dr Seuss makes reading fun, but as we'll see, reading and fun have very little to do with literature.
	(COACH *exits. During his previous line,* PROFESSOR *has searched his pockets unsuccessfully for his papers.*)
	Shoot, I left my papers –
MATT	Oh, I'll get them, Professor.
	(*He exits.*)
PROFESSOR	Thank you, Matthew. You see, I've made it my life's work to create a collection of the world's great poems. And as well-read members of society, you need to be familiar with such luminary poets as Yeats, Keats, Longfellow,

Tennyson, Maya Angelou, TS Eliot, Walt Whitman, The Brothers Gibb . . .

(MATT *runs on, hands several sheets of paper to* PROFESSOR.)

MATT There you go, Professor.

(MATT *goes to the bookcase to straighten up.*)

PROFESSOR Ah, thank you, Matthew. Ladies and gentlemen, my humble collection of the World's Great Poems. (*clears his throat and begins to declaim*) "Toilet paper, extra large Nivea hand lo–" What is this?

(MATT *runs down to him.*)

MATT No, no! Don't read that. That's my shopping list. Professor do me a favour, do not read that!

(MATT *exits.*)

PROFESSOR Matthew, this is not what I need. I need my collection of poems. (*As he says this, he rips the pages three times and tosses them in the air.*)

MATT (*off*) Your collection of poems is on the back!

(PROFESSOR *stares at the papers fluttering to the floor, as the lights shift to a spotlight on him.*)

PROFESSOR Don't worry. It's all up here. (*He taps his head, then stands there for a surprisingly long moment, convinced that something will come to him. Finally, something does.*) There once was a man from Nantucket . . .

(*The audience laughs.* PROFESSOR *goes on, making it up as he goes.*)

Whose string was so long he could pluck it
He shot an arrow in the air
It fell to Earth, there's no there there
And in the depths of his despair cried, "Fuh –

(*He catches himself and finds a different f-word to say.*)

– fie on the person who put me here

In the Ballad of Reading Gaol
Where each man kills the thing he loves
And loves the thing he nails."

(*He realizes that was horribly wrong.*)

Oh . . . Captain! My Captain!

(*He slowly drops to one knee, trying to pick up a paper scrap without being seen.*)

We go down to the sea in ships . . .

(*He stands confidently, reading the only line on the tiny scrap of paper.*)

The rhyming ancient mariner stormed the beach!

(*He realizes he's got nothing – again. He drops to his knee to search for scraps and remembers another phrase.*)

"Beware the Jabberwock, my son
Who dares to part his hair behind . . .

(*He finds two other scraps and reads triumphantly from one of them.*)

And in Xanadu did Kubla Khan dare to eat a –

(*Switching to the other scrap.*)

Peach, bananas, cucumbers, lettuce . . .

(He realizes he's reading from the wrong side of the paper. He flips it over and continues, getting on a roll.)

Let us go, then, you and I
When evening is spread out amongst the sky
Sky light burning bright
First star I see tonight
Rage rage against the dying of the light . . .

(Standing triumphantly.)

Do not go gentle into Gladys Knight!
Two roads diverged in a wood today
How do I love thee? Let me count the way
And I think that I shall never see
A poem as lovely as Doris Day . . .

(Or Beyoncé, or Rachel Ray, or any other celebrety whose surname rhymes with the word 'way'.)

Into the valley of the dolls rode the six hundred
On the eighteenth of April in seventy-five
Seventy-six trombones led the big parade
And I was stayin' alive, stayin' alive
O body swayed to music, O brightening glance
How can we know the dancer from the dance?
I know why the caged bird sings the body electric
Like a maniac, a maniac . . .

(He kneels.)

On the floor!

(Referring to the torn papers on the floor.)

These were my North, my South,
My East, my West,
My noonday lunch, my brekky-fest.
My thoughts are ugly dark and deep
(Referring to MATT.*)* I'd like to choke that little
                                            creep

But I cannot for t'would be a sin.
But when your memory's betrayed you
If you don't curse the god that made you
You're a better man than I am,
Rin Tin Tin." (*Or Ho Chi Minh.*)

Thank you.

(*He nods his head humbly.* COACH *and* MATT *re-enter, applauding. The lights come up.*)

MATT Wow! Good save, Professor.

PROFESSOR Not much of a "collection". More of a "medley", really.

MATT No, no, well done, man. Totally excrement.

PROFESSOR (*thrilled, thinking he said 'excellent'*) Thank you.

MATT You know, I hate to bring this up but I'm a little concerned that this course is focusing only on dead white men.

PROFESSOR That's a fair concern, Matthew, but don't worry, we've addressed this. Next semester I'll be teaching a course on "The Great Works by Trans-Gendered Lesbian Authors of Colour." Please sign up, it'll be held upstairs in the broom closet. And secondly, Alexander Dumas is on the syllabus. And he wasn't white, he was black.

MATT Professor, please! Don't say "black." Say "African-American."

PROFESSOR But he was French.

MATT Then say, "Franco-American."

PROFESSOR Okay. Alexander Dumas: the author of *The Count of Monte Cristo* and *The Three*

	Musketeers was not white – ah! (*Remembering.*) And neither was Homer.
MATT	That's right. Homer's yellow. And his wife had big blue hair. And his son is named Bart –
COACH/ PROFESSOR	Matt!
PROFESSOR	Not *that* Homer. Homer, the Greek poet. Many scholars now believe that Homer was African. *African*-African. At the very least he was Greek, so he was dark and swarthy-looking. Well, he was from Greece, so he was Greece-y. Like Italians!
MATT/COACH	Professor! Mr Tichenor!
PROFESSOR	(*completely flustered*) Ah, I – Look, I don't want to talk about skin colour, I want to focus on the work! But since we're on the subject, I'll grant you that James Joyce was an Irish cream and Leo Tolstoy a white Russian. But Lady Murasaki is obviously not a dead white man. She was the Japanese noblewoman who in the tenth century wrote *The Story of Ghenji*, the world's first novel.
	(COACH *heads to the board and erases everything on it.*)
COACH	The second-best book on the syllabus was written by a woman.
MATT	Who's that, Coach?
COACH	Louisa May Alcott.
PROFESSOR	You think *Little Women*'s a good book?
COACH	*Au contraire mon petite fromage. Little Women* is a great book. Now in the book *Little Women*, the mother is named Marmee – which is short for "marmalade," because she's an

extremely sweet woman, as well as the team's coach and manager, and she's assembled a very strong squad . . .

(*Across the top of the board he writes the first initials of the following names on the board.*)

. . . with Meg, Amy, Beth, Edith, Tamara, Venus, Serena, and Flo Jo – the book's narrator. As the novel begins, the Little Women have lost their best player, their father . . .

(*He writes a small 'F'.*)

. . . to free agency. The American Civil War has broken out and he's signed with the Yankees. The Little Women are now a player down. Fortunately, the boy Laurie lives next door.

(*He writes an 'L'.*)

He's an orphan, a free agent. The Little Women sign him and the league allows it because, let's face it, Laurie – girl's name. At this point the Little Women get two pieces of bad news. First they learn that Beth . . .

(*He circles the letter "B" and then draws a downward line, at the end of which he draws a circle.*)

. . . has run to the sidelines to help the down and out family down the street whose infant has scarlet fever. Beth herself catches scarlet fever and is penalized with a red card . . .

(*He draws eyes and a frown inside the circle to make it a sad face.*)

. . . and her life.

(*He makes an 'X' across the sad face, crossing it out.*)

They also learn that their father has taken ill and been placed on the Disabled List. At this point the Little Women re-acquire the Father, nurse him back to health by pumping him full of steroids . . .

(*He draws a huge exaggerated 'F' next to the smaller one he drew earlier.*)

. . . and he goes on to win the Golden Boot, as the Little Women win the World Cup.

(*He writes "Win" on the board.*)

Now, the Little Women are so successful because their four best players are . . . (*He writes the first initials of these four names from last to first, so they spell out the word "Team."*) Meg, Amy, Edith and Tamara. That's right. There's no "I" in "Team," no "U" in "Win." And all the Little Women . . . (*He draws the "female" sign on the board – the circle with a "+" at the bottom – and then turns it into a happy face.*) . . . live happily ever after. I thank you.

(PROFESSOR *shakes* COACH'*s hand.* MATT *runs on wearing a straw hat.*)

MATT	Yee-haw!! I'm gonna take my raft down the Mississippi River!
COACH	Woah! Matt, we're not doing *Huck Finn*!
PROFESSOR	What?!
MATT	What are you talking about? Ernest Hemingway said that all American literature stems from *Huckleberry Finn*!

PROFESSOR	He's right, Coach. And *Huckleberry Finn* is great source material for dramatisation.
COACH	Yes, but we don't have the right people for *Huck Finn*.
MATT	We don't have the right people for any of these books.
COACH	No, you're missing my point. Who's gonna play Jim?
MATT	I don't know. Why don't you play Jim? You're big.
COACH	I'm not black.
MATT	Oh my god, that is so racist!
PROFESSOR	No, it isn't.
MATT	Yes, it is. He just denied himself an opportunity because of his race!
COACH	No, Jim was African-American. He was a runaway slave, not a runaway Scottish-German-Presbyterian. (*Indicating himself. The actor playing this role should say his own actual ethnicity and religion.*)
MATT	What kind of logic is that? C'mon Professor, you've heard of colour-blind casting, haven't you?
PROFESSOR	You forget, I directed the first all-white production of *Porgy and Bess* (*Or whatever show your audience would be familiar with that couldn't possibly have an all-white cast*). So you can play Jim.
COACH	Okay, I'll agree to play Jim if you two agree we'll be true to the original language.
PROFESSOR	Absolutely.

MATT	Why else would you do it?
	(PROFESSOR *and* MATT *start to exit.*)
COACH	So we'll be saying the 'N' word?
PROFESSOR	Yes.
MATT	The what?
COACH	The 'N' word.
	(MATT *shrugs.* COACH *whispers the word to* MATT.)
MATT	Oh my god, that is so racist!
PROFESSOR	No, it isn't.
MATT	Did you just hear what he said?!
COACH	I didn't call anybody that, I wasn't referring to anybody. We were having a class discussion, and in that context I'm perfectly comfortable saying it right out loud. You know . . .
	(*He whispers it behind his hand to* MATT.)
MATT	Oh, my god! That is so racist!
PROFESSOR	Matthew, Huck says that word. It's in the book.
MATT	That word is in the book?
PROFESSOR	Yes, it's accurate nineteenth century derogatory slang.
MATT	(*to the class*) Well, then you can cross *Huckleberry Finn* off your syllabus. We're not going to cover it. That book is racist.
PROFESSOR	No!

ACT ONE

MATT
Yes!

PROFESSOR
Matthew, depicting racism is not racist. That's why we should study the book. Because it shows Huck's growing awareness of, and then rejection of, racism.

MATT
Yeah, but I am not comfortable with that word. Coach, I'm not comfortable with any ethnic labels.

COACH
But if we don't use ethnic labels, what do we call them?

MATT
"Them"? "Them"?! How about calling them "people"? Or "fellow human beings"?!

COACH
Calling who?

MATT
"Them"! "Them"! Don't make generalisations based on race. Argh! All white people do that.

(COACH *and* PROFESSOR *look at* MATT, *then continue.*)

PROFESSOR
You know, speaking of ethnic labels, did you know that in England black people are not called African-Americans?

COACH
Really?

MATT
All right. Can we please stop talking about this?

PROFESSOR
Oh, you know what they call underwear in England?

COACH
No.

MATT
Stop talking about black people.

PROFESSOR
Knickers.

COACH	Oh!
MATT	Oh my god, that's so racist!
	(MATT *begins to leave.*)
COACH	Oh, you know what they call a sausage in England?
PROFESSOR	No.
MATT	I'm calling my wife.
	(MATT *begins to leave again.*)
COACH	Banger.
PROFESSOR	Right.
MATT	Hey! I said *call* my wife!
PROFESSOR	You know what they call a cigarette in England?
COACH	Yep.
MATT	(*still trying to leave*) I'm telling my mom!
COACH/ PROFESSOR	Fag!
MATT	Hey! That was one time! In college! And I was drunk!
	(*Slowly,* MATT *realizes he may have revealed too much.*)
PROFESSOR	What, you smoked a cigarette?
MATT	Afterwards. Look, I don't understand how my personal life got on the syllabus. Can we please get back to *Huckleberry Finn?* The story of America, an adolescent country

dealing with its ethics, morality, coming of age and in the end ultimately finding redemption?

(*Beat.*)

PROFESSOR Wow. That is an excellent summation of *Huckleberry Finn*.

MATT Wow? You don't have to be so surprised, Professor!

PROFESSOR I'm sorry. It's just that, basically, I've always thought you were illiterate.

(MATT *charges the* PROFESSOR, *who runs away.* COACH *restrains* MATT.)

MATT I'll rip your head off!

COACH Hey, Matt, calm down!

MATT I am not illiterate! My parents were married!

PROFESSOR I didn't mean you were born out of wedlock, I meant you can't read or write.

MATT Course I can read and write! Just because I'm a student teacher doesn't make me a *total* idiot.

PROFESSOR All right, I'm sorry I called you illiterate.

MATT You should be! You should also be sorry for this, ah-ha! (*He pulls a book out of the back of his trousers.*) I found this in the garbage!

PROFESSOR What is it?

MATT It's *Walden* by Henry David Thoreau and *you* threw it away!

PROFESSOR Oh, I did not!

(*The* PROFESSOR *exits. The scene continues on page 22.*) [*Now, if there's something political going on in the news, you can do this Breakdown Section. In this scenario,* PROFESSOR *doesn't say his "I didn't mean you were born out of wedlock . . ." line. Instead, he hides behind the American flag after* MATT'S *"My parents were married" line, and it goes like this:]*

MATT   Just because I'm a student teacher doesn't make me . . . Stop that. What are you – ? Come out of . . . stop hiding behind the flag.

PROFESSOR   (*stepping out*) Why? It seems to be working for President Bush. (*Or whichever politician is deflecting criticism by questioning other people's patriotism.*)

MATT   Stop that . . .

(*The audience will have a mixed response to this. To gauge whether he's gone too far,* PROFESSOR *can simulate a laugh-meter with his arms.*)

Hey, you guys are the teachers. I guess you can go wherever you want.

PROFESSOR   (*back in character*) All right, I'm sorry I called you illiterate.

MATT   (*thrown*) No, uh. You . . . hmm . . . what? (*He tries to pick up the scene from where it left off, but can't remember what he's supposed to say.*)

COACH   I guess because we're the teachers, that explains why we know where we are.

(*The audience laughs.* MATT *has to acknowledge that* COACH *got him, but still defend himself.*)

MATT   (*sotto voce*) All right. Okay. But he said that, you said that already.

PROFESSOR (*sotto voce*) I said it but I didn't apologize for it . . .

COACH (*sotto voce*) Matt, pull the book out of your pants.

MATT What? Right. Skip it. (*Pulls book from the back of his trousers.*) Aha! Look what I found!

PROFESSOR Where'd you pull that out from?

MATT Stop it! I'm trying to get back to the . . . Ah-ha! Look I what found in the –

COACH (*to the audience leading the applause*) Matt Croke, ladies and gentlemen!

MATT No, come on, stop. There's a rhythm to this, guys, a rhythm!

COACH (*looking at his watch*) Not for the last fifteen minutes.

MATT I found this in the garbage! Yeah, I'm really mad now!

PROFESSOR What is it?

MATT Oh, you know what it is! It's *Walden* by Henry David Thoreau, and you threw it away.

PROFESSOR I did not.

(PROFESSOR *exits. And now you're back to the script.*)

MATT Oh my gosh. Coach, Professor threw *Walden* in the garbage.

COACH Professor didn't throw *Walden* in the garbage, I did. Because absolutely nothing happens in that book.

MATT	But this is *Walden*. It's a great book! It's a manifesto for non-violent social change that inspired Ghandi and Martin Luther King.
COACH	It's about a guy sitting by a pond contemplating his navel.
MATT	But I have an action packed interpretation that I do with a subtle beauty.
COACH	Well, it's on the syllabus but make it quick.

(MATT *hands the book to* COACH *and goes to grab the chair.*)

Ladies and gentlemen, finally, an action packed, subtle interpretation of Henry David Thoreau's *Walden.*

(*The lights shift.* MATT *has moved the chair downstage and sits on it, in a spotlight. We hear gentle music and sounds of crickets and sparrows.* MATT *sits very still. After a while, he swats away an imaginary fly. Then he picks up an imaginary fishing pole and mimes casting the line into the pond. Suddenly* COACH *blows his whistle. The lights bounce back up.*)

(*Using the actual American football referee signals for "Personal Foul" and "Intentional Grounding".*) Personal foul. Intentionally boring.

MATT	What are you talking about?
COACH	Yeah, there's a subtle beauty. So subtle I can't see it.
MATT	What could be more exciting than *Walden* by Henry David Thoreau?
COACH	*Walden* by Ernest Hemingway.

(COACH *slaps the book into* MATT'S *chest. The lights shift again to just the spotlight. We again hear the gentle music and sounds of crickets and sparrows.* COACH *turns his baseball cap backwards and sits in the chair. He mimes taking a flask out of his pocket and taking a deep drink. He tosses the flask aside. Then he mimes casting and fishing. The pole breaks, so* COACH *mimes grabbing a rifle. He shoots toward the wings.* MATT *runs on carrying a very large bucket and large stuffed fish. He deliberately sets down the bucket, drops the fish in it and exits.* COACH *is puzzled, but then takes aim at something overhead and shoots. A second large fish falls from the sky and drops directly into the bucket.* COACH *looks at the audience and gets an idea. He raises one eyebrow. Blackout. Lights up.* MATT *restores the chair.* PROFESSOR *enters checking his syllabus.*)

Guys, we need to pick up the tempo here. We still have all these books to cover. I say we just jump right into *War and Peace*. (*He picks up the huge War and Peace book.*)

PROFESSOR
Woah! Coach, don't you think *War and Peace* is a little complicated?

COACH
What's complicated? It's just like every other Russian novel. The motherland is being invaded, the people are being persecuted, and the Russians are drunk off their ass. (*He slams the huge War and Peace book shut and sets it back down on the floor.*)

MATT
You know what? Nobody knows the Russian novels. Why don't we cover a book that everybody has read?

PROFESSOR
Good thinking, Matthew. Here's one I'm sure you all know. (*Picking one off the floor.*) How many of you have read *Don Quixote*?

(The three performers raise their hands, indicating that anyone who has read Don Quixote should raise theirs. Hardly anyone does.)

COACH   Seven.

MATT   What?

PROFESSOR   Come on! You must know the musical *Man of La Mancha*. *(Singing very, very badly.)* To dream, the impossible – !

MATT/COACH   *(various)* Woah! Hey! Stop!

COACH   Mr Tichenor, that's okay!

PROFESSOR   But I love that song!

COACH   Well then learn the tune.

PROFESSOR   *Don Quixote*'s a great story, all about an old man who imagines himself to be a knight errant! Where we see windmills, Don Quixote sees giants.

COACH   Where we see prostitutes, he sees princesses.

MATT   Where we see Jim Carrey, he sees Antonio Banderas.

COACH/PROFESSOR   *Si!*

(The guys clap twice in unison, as if they're flamenco dancers. PROFESSOR tosses MATT the book, which MATT places on the bookshelf upstage as he and COACH exit. PROFESSOR moves up near the door as he speaks.)

PROFESSOR   *Don Quixote* is an exquisite story all about the power of the imagination! In Don Quixote's world, this tattered robe –

(From offstage someone throws Professor *a worn-out looking bathrobe. He catches it and puts it on.)*

– becomes a magnificent suit of armor. And this child's plaything –

(On flies a plastic pail, which he puts on his head, tucking the handle under his chin.)

– becomes a knight's helmet. Now in order for you to more fully appreciate the beauty inherent in Miguel de Cervantes' language, my extinguished colleague Coach will join me in performing *Don Quixote* in the original Spanish, while Matthew translates.

*(*Matt *enters and crosses to a spot DL.)*

MATT: Hola. *(He waves.)* Hello. *(He waves.)*

*(*Professor *poses dramatically.)*

PROFESSOR/QUIXOTE: *Soy Don Quixote de la Mancha.*

MATT: I am Don Quixote of La Mancha.

PROFESSOR/QUIXOTE: *. . . el desachador de injusticia . . .*

MATT: . . . the undoer of injustice . . .

PROFESSOR/QUIXOTE: *. . . el protector de doncellas . . .*

MATT: . . . the protector of damsels . . .

PROFESSOR/QUIXOTE: *. . . y el terror de gigantes.*

MATT: . . . and the terror of giants.

PROFESSOR/QUIXOTE: *Montaré mi magnifico caballo, Rocinante.*

MATT	I will ride on my magnificent horse, Rocinante.

(PROFESSOR *looks to the doorway, anticipating that he will be thrown a stick horse. But instead of being thrown onstage, the stick horse is "accidentally" thrown across the doorway and out of sight upstage. After a beat, we see an embarrassed stage hand cross the doorway to retrieve the stick horse. After another beat, the stage hand crosses back to his original position. Finally,* PROFESSOR *says . . .*)

PROFESSOR/ QUIXOTE	*Rocinante!*

(*A hand holds out the stick horse from the doorway.* PROFESSOR *takes it and puts it between his legs, but with the horse's face facing up. He does a double-take at the horse and then turns the head so that it faces downward.* COACH *enters, riding a mop like a stick donkey. He speaks with a heavily nasal Mexican accent.*)

COACH/SANCHO	Hola, Señor Quixado. Me llamo Sancho Panza. Como esta?
MATT	(*imitating his accent*) Good morning, Mr. Quixado. My name is Sancho Panza. How are you?
PROFESSOR/ QUIXOTE	*No soy Señor Quixado. Soy Don Quixote de la Mancha.*
MATT	I am not Mister Quixado. I am Don Quixote of La Mancha.
PROFESSOR/ QUIXOTE	*Yo requiero un escudero fiel para mi pesquisa.*
MATT	I require a faithful squire for my quest.

PROFESSOR/ *Me acompañas?*
QUIXOTE

MATT   Will you join me?

COACH/SANCHO *No se.*

MATT   (*exaggerating* COACH's *accent*) I'm not sure.

PROFESSOR/   *Qiuero hacer bien . . .*
QUIXOTE

MATT   I want to do right . . .

PROFESSOR/   *. . . a los hechos malos . . .*
QUIXOTE

MATT   . . . to right wrongs . . .

PROFESSOR/   *. . . y impresionar Dulcinea . . .*
QUIXOTE

MATT   . . . and to win the love of Dulcinea . . .

PROFESSOR/   *. . . la chica con los melones mas grandes en*
QUIXOTE   *Espana.*

              (*He gestures, indicating large breasts.* MATT
              *is shocked and doesn't quite know how to
              translate this, but finally . . .*)

MATT   (*repeating* PROFESSOR's *gesture*) . . . the girl
              with the biggest hands in Spain.

COACH/SANCHO *Si, te acompañares en tu sueño imposible.*

MATT   Yes, I will join you in your impossible dream.

COACH/SANCHO *Pero tengo miedo que yo no pueda marchar al
              paso de un asno de este tamaño.*

MATT   But I'm afraid that I will not be able to keep
              pace with an ass of this size.

(PROFESSOR *and* MATT *look at* COACH's *behind.* COACH *turns and looks at the wall, then shrugs and continues.*)

COACH/SANCHO *Y como fue que Mateo pudo hacer todo en ingles?*

MATT And how come Matt gets to do the whole scene in English?

PROFESSOR/QUIXOTE *Porque Mateo es estupido.*

(PROFESSOR *and* COACH *have a good laugh.*)

MATT Because Matt is stupendous. (*Quickly repeating his waves.*) Hola! Hello!

PROFESSOR/QUIXOTE *Andale!*

MATT Let's ride!

(PROFESSOR *and* COACH *"ride" in a half circle around the stage.* PROFESSOR *makes horse noises,* COACH *makes donkey sounds.* MATT *slaps his chest to make galloping sounds.*)

PROFESSOR/QUIXOTE *Alto!*

MATT Stop!

PROFESSOR/QUIXOTE *Mira, amigo Sancho! Gigantes!*

MATT Look, friend Sancho! Giants!

COACH/SANCHO *Usted es loco. Todo lo que veo son molinos de viento.*

MATT You are delusional, my friend. All I see are windmills.

PROFESSOR/ QUIXOTE *No estoy loco!*

MATT Sanity is overrated!

COACH/SANCHO *Pardoname.*

MATT I'm sorry.

COACH/SANCHO *Mi mal.*

MATT My bad.

PROFESSOR/ QUIXOTE *Gracias.*

MATT Thank you.

COACH (*very angrily, to* MATT) They know what *gracias* means.

MATT (*imitating* COACH, *very angrily*) *Saben que quiere decir "gracias."*

(COACH *and* PROFESSOR *turn slowly and stare angrily at* MATT. MATT *shrugs as if to say, "What? They liked it."*)

PROFESSOR/ QUIXOTE *Tengo que atacar! Ha, ha!*

MATT I must attack! Hee, hee!

(PROFESSOR *rides through the doorway. We hear and see bits of a struggle.* PROFESSOR'S *head sticks out and a huge green toy Hulk hand grabs it and pulls it back.* (*In fact, he himself is wearing the green toy Hulk hand.*) *Then the stick horse's head sticks out and looks at the audience with a confused Scooby sound. The hand appears and pulls the head back with a loud "Zoinks!". Then* PROFESSOR *crosses past the doorway with his own hands around his throat.*)

PROFESSOR/ QUIXOTE	*Oh, dios mio!*
MATT	Oh, my God.
	(*Now* PROFESSOR *passes back across the doorway, dragging himself by his own pink sweater vest. As he disappears there's a loud thud.*)
PROFESSOR/ QUIXOTE	(*off*) *Oh, mi cajones!*
MATT	Oh, my testicles.
	(PROFESSOR *stumbles back on, holding his crotch.*)
COACH/SANCHO	*Como estas, Don Quixote?*
PROFESSOR/ QUIXOTE	*No muy bueno.*
MATT	(*as* COACH) How are you, Don Quixote? (*As* PROFESSOR, *high-pitched.*) Not very well.
COACH/SANCHO	*Tuviste una pelea falsa contigo mismo de fuera del escenario.*
MATT	You had a very phony fight with yourself offstage.
PROFESSOR/ QUIXOTE	*No es phonisimo. Es muy realistico.*
MATT	It was not phony. It was very realistic.
PROFESSOR/ QUIXOTE	*Estaba peliando con gigantes . . .*
MATT	I was battling giants . . .
PROFESSOR/ QUIXOTE	*. . . en las planos de España.*

MATT ... on the plains of Spain.

COACH/SANCHO *Donde hay lluvia?*

MATT Where the rain mainly stays?

(COACH *smiles at his own cleverness.*)

PROFESSOR (*smiling to disguise how angry he is*) *Hijo de puta!*

(MATT *is instantly shocked.* COACH *doesn't know what it means and looks over for the translation.*)

MATT He questions Sancho's heritage.

(COACH *is angered.*)

PROFESSOR/QUIXOTE *Chinga té!*

(COACH *again looks to* MATT *for the translation.*)

MATT And tells him to perform a physical impossibility on himself.

PROFESSOR/QUIXOTE (*referring to the mop donkey*) *Y tu burro, tambien.*

MATT And the horse he rode in on.

PROFESSOR/QUIXOTE *Y tú! Chinga té, tambien!*

(*He gives the "up yours" sign to* MATT, *and storms off.*)

MATT (*repeating the "up yours" gesture*) And he salutes me for all my work on this difficult translation.

(COACH *follows the* PROFESSOR *off.*)

Gracias.

(MATT *bows. He looks off.*)

I hope Coach doesn't hit the Professor. Coach is a great guy and all but he's got a bit of a temper, its kind of legendary.

(*He waits for a beat, hoping they'll re-appear. When they don't, he decides to take charge.*)

Actually, you know what will make him really mad? I used to do this when I went to school here. This is great. (*He picks up a book.*) Oh perfect – Plato's *Republic*. When Coach says the word "Plato," everybody sneeze. Okay? This'll be great. When you hear "Plato," sneeze. Got it? Now Coach might get so upset that he'll forget to cover Plato, but don't worry about it. I'll cover it for you now, just in case. He's only one guy, how tough can it be.

(*He flips through the book. It looks incomprehensible so he figures it must be upside down. He flips it over. Then he realizes he had it right the first time and flips it back.*)

Now we all know that Plato wrote a lot of great books, but what he's really best known for is that soft molding clay that bears his name.

(COACH *re-enters.*)

COACH Everything under control?

MATT Yeah, Coach. Great class.

COACH Sorry for the interruption, students. Mr Tichenor?

(PROFESSOR *enters, holding an ice pack to his crotch.*)

There we are. Is this the next book?

(MATT *hands him the Plato book.*)

MATT
Yes it is, Coach. All set.

COACH
(*opening the book*) Ah yes. The great Greek philosopher, Plato.

(*The class sneezes in unison.*)

All right. Who's behind this?

PROFESSOR
Come on, Coach. You need to have a sense of humour about this sort of thing. Little scamps.

COACH
You know, you screw around for four years of high school . . . (*Picking someone specific, like a latecomer if there was one.*) In some cases, seven years . . .

MATT
Coach, how about if I form a committee, and I'll find out who did this.

COACH
I like the way you think.

MATT
Yes sir!

COACH
(*opening the book again*) Now, we all know that the great Greek philosopher Plato wrote a lot of . . .

(*The class sneezes again.* COACH *slams the book to the floor and tries to charge into the class.* PROFESSOR *and* MATT *restrain him.*)

This is ridiculous! I am trying to teach a class!

PROFESSOR
Coach, you need to learn to laugh at yourself.

MATT	Coach, c'mon. Besides, I've covered all this already.
PROFESSOR	Wait. You covered the great Greek philosopher Plato?!

(*The class sneezes, with any luck.* PROFESSOR *turns on them.*)

That's not funny!

MATT	(*to the class*) What is wrong with you people? I said when Coach says it.

(COACH *and* PROFESSOR *slowly turn to look at him.*)

COACH	WHAT!?!?!
MATT	(*covering*) That's right. I said when Coach says it, you do it! If he says jump, you ask "How high?"
COACH	All right!
MATT	Yeah!

(COACH *and* MATT *high five.* MATT *hurts his hand. He places the Plato book on the bookshelf and exits.*)

PROFESSOR	Well, if Matthew's already covered Plato . . .

(*If the class sneezes here,* PROFESSOR *gives them a disdainful "Stop it."*)

. . . then the only ancient left on the syllabus is my favorite author, the Greek poet Homer. Now, Homer wrote and performed the two epics that are the basis for all Western literature – *The Iliad* and *The Odyssey* – which I have translated from the original Greek into rhyming iambic septameter.

(MATT *returns with three copies of the* PROFESSOR'S *translation and hands one to* PROFESSOR *and one to* COACH.)

Thank you, Matthew. Now in my translation, you're playing the great Greek warrior Achilles.

MATT
Awesome! Achilles! He's the ... uh ...

COACH
He's the hero of *The Iliad*.

MATT
Right! I love *The Iliad* ... the epic story of – ?

PROFESSOR
Of Achilles, who is sent off to rescue Helen of Troy and ultimately changes the course of the Trojan War.

MATT
Right, this'll be fun. Remind me again, what's his background?

PROFESSOR
Oh this is good. When Achilles was a baby, his mother dipped him into the River Styx ...

MATT
That's terrible!

PROFESSOR
No, no – to make him invincible.

MATT
Awesome!

PROFESSOR
But she held him by the heel, which did not get wet, so that part remained vulnerable. It's from this we get the term "Achilles heel".

MATT
So except for my heel, nobody can see me!

COACH/
PROFESSOR
No! No!

(MATT *starts to act like* PROFESSOR *and* COACH *can't see him. He makes ghost sounds and pretends to float. He picks up a book and acts like it's floating on its own, then he carries it up to the doorway and drops it on the bookshelf. He exits.*)

COACH (*following* MATT *off*) I'll make sure he doesn't disappear.

PROFESSOR Thank you. Now, this godfather of all literary journeys must begin with the traditional invocation to the Greek gods.

(*He sticks the script in his pocket and claps his hands. The lights snap to a special. He adopts an invocation pose.*)

Oh, muse of epic poetry, Calliope by name
Please grant my new translation with a measure of your fame
And help us understand Homer's *Iliad* and *Odyssey*
Through my humbly brilliant version, called "The Idioddity!"

(*Dramatic music begins.* PROFESSOR *exits as* COACH *enters. He reads his script.*)

COACH/CHORUS Achilles was a soldier, Agamemnon was his king
They both were given women, which are very special things
But Agamemnon gave his back. That's the kind of King he is.
And since he gave his back, he thought Achilles should give him his.

(MATT *enters in Achilles breast plate. He carries a small spear.*)

MATT/ACHILLES That is an insult! I won that woman fair and square! I'm Achilles! When I was a baby, I was dipped in the River Styx, now nobody can see me. I am invisible!

COACH/CHORUS Achilles stopped participating in the Trojan War.

MATT/ACHILLES I do not hate the Trojans so what am I fighting for?

COACH/CHORUS Athena then appeared, she was beautiful and mincing,

>   (PROFESSOR *"floats" on, in a wig and large hoop skirt. The skirt is floor length, so it covers his feet. He appears to be floating.*)

And here's what's kinda scary. He's surprisingly convincing. (*He exits.*)

PROFESSOR/ATHENA Achilles, don't! Agamemnon is your king and fellow Greek!

MATT/ACHILLES But he's insulted me and made me look feeble and weak!

PROFESSOR/ATHENA You can't withdraw! He needs your skill to fight the Trojan War.

MATT/ACHILLES Well, all that I can say is he shoulda thoughta that before.

>   (MATT *stabs the hoop skirt and exits. The hoop skirt starts to "deflate" like all the air is escaping from under it.*)

PROFESSOR Ahhhhh! I'm melting, I'm MELTING!

>   (*He "melts" slowly to the floor. When he gets as low as he can, he bows and exits.*)

Thank you.

>   (*And, thus, we cover* The Wizard of Oz. COACH *enters.*)

COACH/CHORUS Achilles couldn't help it. The Gods' mighty magic laws
Fueled his pride and anger.

>   (MATT *pops his head back out.*)

MATT/ACHILLES I hate my tragic flaws!

COACH/CHORUS Now comes Paris, the most hated person on the planet

> (COACH *exits. The* PROFESSOR *enters in a beret, twirling a plastic sword.*)

PROFESSOR/PARIS Ohh, ho, ho, ho!
You know zat 'orrible Trojan War? Well, I began it.
Zis is Helen of Troy, ze greatest beauty of our day.

> (MATT *re-enters as* HELEN OF TROY, *with wig, skirt and feather boa.*)

MATT/HELEN My face launched a thousand ships!

PROFESSOR/PARIS Zey couldn't wait to get away.
Zis whole war started when I stole her from Menolaos,
Which is why he and all ze Greeks now want to slay us.

> (COACH *enters with crown, plastic sword, and glasses.*)

COACH/MENALAOS I'm Menalaos. That's my wife. Now what do you propose?

PROFESSOR/PARIS A duel between us will bring years of fighting to a close.

MATT/HELEN And the winner of this battle gets to take off all my clothes!

> (MATT *exits.*)

COACH/MENALAOS I accept your challenge, and will avenge what you did to me.

> (*They draw their swords.*)

PROFESSOR/PARIS If you want your wife back, sucker, you will have to go right through me!

(MENALAOS *lightly taps* PARIS *on the arm*.)

Ow! I'm hit! Great Zeus! I am feeling very sickly!

(PROFESSOR *exits*.)

COACH/
MENALAOS Leave it to a Frenchman to surrender very quickly.

(COACH *exits*. MATT *enters as* CHORUS.)

MATT/CHORUS And so the war continued, many thousands more were dying
King Agamemnon couldn't win –

(COACH *enters*. MATT *leaves*.)

COACH/
AGAMEMNON Hey, at least I'm trying!

(*The* PROFESSOR *enters, doing his own fanfare. He wear a blue t-shirt with a Greek "O" (Omega) sign on the front. It looks like the "S" logo that Superman wears. The shirt has a short red cape attached*.)

PROFESSOR/
ODYSSEUS I'm Odysseus, your highness, let me go to Troy and check it.
I'll reconnoiter.

COACH/
AGAMEMNON Good. You find that noiter and you wreck it!

(COACH *exits*.)

PROFESSOR/
ODYSSUS I will.
That night we crept to town and we made the Trojans blee-id
In the only section in this class you'll hear from *The Aeneid*.

(The class reacts to the bad rhyme. PROFESSOR drops his Odysseus character.)

PROFESSOR   All right, you just bought yourselves a lecture. *The Aeneid* is the Roman poet Virgil's story about the founding of Rome. It too tells the story of the Trojan War, but more from the viewpoint of Roman nationalism. The lesson here is that the Romans stole everything from the Greeks: their Gods, their myths, their salads. So we're gonna skip *The Aeneid*, except for this famous section, which I'm sure you'll recognize. *(Back in character.)*
I gathered all my men in a large and rather coarse group
And entered through the main gate disguised as Trojan Horse poop.

(He exits. Music plays. COACH and MATT enter in a vaudeville horse costume. COACH is the head; MATT'S the rear end. They sneak around in time to the music. PROFESSOR enters as a guard who keeps looking for the horse, but not seeing it. Finally the guard spots the horse, who hands the guard a scroll that says, "For The Trojans." The guard shows the note to the audience, gestures to the horse to follow him into the city, then skips offstage. The horse does a little celebratory dance, finishing with step-kicks and a bow. PROFESSOR re-enters as ODYSSEUS, hiding upstage of the horse. He crawls underneath the horse and speaks.)

PROFESSOR/   Once they got me in I couldn't wait to go get
ODYSSIUS   started!
This really was a master plan

MATT   *(taking off his part of the horse costume)* All right! Who farted?

(MATT exits. COACH, still wearing the horse head, does a slow take to the audience then

sprints off. PROFESSOR *shakes his head: apparently this wasn't planned, and his anger fuels the next line.*)

PROFESSOR/ODYSSIUS This war really stinks. Achilles has to reconsider. His selfishness has made him very angry, very bitter.

(PROFESSOR *exits as* MATT *enters.*)

MATT/ACHILLES Perhaps my foolish arrogance and pride was the cause. I'll ask my trusted friend and adviser, Patroklos! (*Patra-Claus.*)

(COACH *enters as* PATROKLOS. *He wears a red Santa hat and white beard, but still has on the horse trousers. He holds a plastic sword.*)

COACH/PATROKLOS Ho, ho, ho! Merry Iliad, everybody! Hey, little fella have a seat. Tell old Patroklos what you'd like for Christmas.

(MATT *sits on* COACH'S *knee and starts to say his next line, but taps* COACH *on the chest with his spear, then catches his beard with the sword as he pulls it away. They both fall out of character.*)

COACH Ow! You're on the naughty list!

(*He hits* MATT'S *breast plate with his sword then notices that the armour is on back to front.*)

And your armour's on backwards, genius.

MATT At least I managed to get out of my horse pants. Oops!

(COACH *looks down at the horse pants he is indeed still wearing and shakes his head. Then they get back to the scene.*)

COACH	These costume changes are a bitch, folks.
MATT/ACHILLES	(*back in character*) Be careful, Patroklos, there are spies in my house!
COACH/PATROKLOS	No, no! Not a creature is stirring, not even a mouse.
MATT/ACHILLES	My Greeks are getting killed out there. Have I been led astray? What can I do?
COACH/PATROKLOS	My friend, I do believe there is a way! Make a list, check it twice, kill the naughty, save the nice. Let me wear your armor, everyone will think I'm you. The troops will rally 'round me
MATT/ACHILLES	That's the perfect thing to do!

(COACH *puts on* MATT'S *breast plate and begins to exit.*)

And I heard him exclaim as he went off to fight . . .

COACH/PATROKLOS	Merry Battles to all, and to all a good – (*He says half-heartedly from offstage.*) – God I'm being killed!

(*The Santa hat and beard fly out from the doorway where* COACH *exited.* MATT *falls to the ground in over-the-top emotional agony.*)

MATT/ACHILLES	Oh my God, I killed him! In Hell I will be fried! Patraklos is dead! I've committed Patra-cide!

(COACH *enters.*)

COACH/CHORUS	Achilles vows to end the war before there dies another, So he fights with Hektor . . .

(PROFESSOR *enters as* HEKTOR, *in the same beret that* PARIS *wore.*)

         ... Paris's older brother.
The Trojan War can be summed up by what
         they represent.

(COACH *exits.* ACHILLES *with his spear and* HEKTOR *with his sword circle each other. They debate while they fight.* MATT *fights like a tough guy.* PROFESSOR *is prissy.*)

MATT/ACHILLES I'm primitive and brutal!

(MATT *lunges at* PROFESSOR.)

PROFESSOR/   I'm a civil government.
HEKTOR

(PROFESSOR *attacks back.*)

MATT/ACHILLES I'm undisciplined, instinctive.

(MATT *swings his spear at* PROFESSOR.)

PROFESSOR/   I am reason, self-control.
HEKTOR

(PROFESSOR *kicks* MATT *in the groin.*)

MATT/ACHILLES It's every man for himself.

PROFESSOR/   No ...
HEKTOR

(*He slaps* MATT *on the head with his sword.*)

    ... it's mankind as a whole.

MATT/ACHILLES This fighting while debating makes me
                                frustrated and weary.

PROFESSOR/   My benevolent ways will win out –
HEKTOR

(MATT *stabs* PROFESSOR.)

So much for that theory.

(*They bow and exit, shaking hands as they go.* COACH *enters.*)

COACH/CHORUS The Trojan War was over, Achilles had no equal,
But *The Iliad* was such a hit Homer had to
                                  write a sequel.
When *The Odyssey* begins, ten more years
                          have now gone by,
And Odysseus's son is one very wimpy guy.

(COACH *exits.* MATT *skips on as* TELEMACHUS, *wearing a beanie with propeller and licking an oversized lollipop. His voice cracks, like a boy whose voice is changing.*)

MATT/TELEMACHUS I am Telemachus and I don't know what to do.
My mother is besieged by men who all are
                                  pitching woo.

(PROFESSOR *and* COACH *lean their heads in one of the doorways. They hold flowers and candy. In unison they say . . .*)

BOTH Telemachus, is your mom home?

(*They both pant, tongues hanging out of their mouths.* MATT *waves them off, and they pop out of sight.*)

MATT/TELEMACHUS Go away!

BOTH Aw!

MATT/TELEMACHUS They want to marry Mom, they think my
                                  father's not alive . . .

(PROFESSOR *"flies" into one doorway. He achieves this by bending at the waist and*

                          *leaning into the doorway – hands in front of
                          him, chest towards the floor. The audience
                          can only see him only from the waist up.)*

PROFESSOR/   They might be right. I don't appear in *The*
ODYSSEUS   *Odyssey* 'till Book Five.

                          *(He does flying bits in the doorway. He waves
                          at the audience. He does a barrel roll. He
                          turns his body so that his chest is facing the
                          audience and moves up and down. He puts his
                          hand to his brow, looking towards the
                          audience.)*

MATT   Professor, what are you doing?

PROFESSOR/   Just using my x-ray vision.
ODYSSEUS

MATT   Professor, get out here and do Book Five.

                          *(*PROFESSOR *mimes shifting into reverse, and
                          backs out of the doorway.* COACH *makes
                          backing-up beeping noises offstage.*
                          PROFESSOR *leaps into the doorway from the
                          opposite side from which he backed up.* MATT
                          exits.)

PROFESSOR/   *(when audience doesn't react)* No, no, hold
ODYSSEUS   your applause.
                          At the beginning of Book Five, I start my epic
                                                                 journey
                          But first, I'm held as prisoner without trial or
                                                                 attorney
                          I'm trapped for seven years on the island of
                                                                Calypso!

                          *(*MATT *re-enters as* CALYPSO *in wig, grass skirt,
                          and seashell bikini top.)*

MATT/CALYPSO   Day-O! Day-ay-ay-oh! The Gods have told me
                                                 to let you go!

(MATT *shimmies, showing the audience his shells and his behind.*)

PROFESSOR/ODYSSEUS Oh Calypso, you turn me on you wild and wanton lass.
I see your sexy seashells and seductive shapely grass.
I must escape this island and begin my odyssey!

(*He starts to go but* MATT *grabs him.*)

MATT/CALYPSO Only after one more night of sexuality!
(*Rubbing* ODYSSEUS'S *chest.*)
You're gonna get it boy, you know it'll be fantastic.

PROFESSOR Stop it, man, you're scaring me. You're too enthusiastic.

(MATT *grabs a wooden slapstick – available at most music stores – from the bookshelf and makes* PROFESSOR *bend over at the waist.*)

MATT/CALYPSO Assume the position like your Greek fraternal brother.

(*He spanks* PROFESSOR *with the slapstick, then exits.* PROFESSOR *backs upstage in the doorway as he speaks.*)

PROFESSOR Thank you, lovely goddess. Please sir, may I have another?

(MATT'S *hand reaches into the doorway and pulls* PROFESSOR *off stage.* COACH *enters with a trident, wearing a snorkle, mask, and kid's safety float around his waist. The float looks like a turtle or something equally childish.*)

COACH/POSEIDON I am Poseidon. With my trident, I am God of water.
I am Zeus's brother, the little mermaid is my daughter.

                    The nymph has freed Odysseus from his sexual
                                                            indenture
                    I think it's time I sent him on a Poseidon
                                                            adventure!

                    (COACH *waves his trident.* PROFESSOR/
                    ODYSSEUS *is pulled onstage and sent flying
                    into the wings. As he crosses the stage he
                    points at an audience member and says:*)

PROFESSOR/   Look! Ernest Borgnine!
ODYSSEUS

                    (PROFESSOR *screams as he exits.* COACH *exits
                    too, as* MATT *enters to narrate.*)

MATT/CHORUS   How did Odysseus, wanting to get home
                                                    despite the odds,
                    Manage to piss off one of the nastiest of Gods?
                    Let's find out. Odysseus washes up in foreign
                                                            territory –

                    (PROFESSOR *"washes up" onto the stage.
                    Unbeknownst to the audience, he has a
                    mouthful of water. Laying on his back, he
                    spits some of it into the air like a fountain. It
                    sprays people in the front row.*)

                    – and proceeds to tell the natives there his
                                                    most amazing story.

                    (COACH *has entered as Phaeacian King*
                    ALCINOUS. *He is hard of hearing and has an
                    ear horn. He, too, has a mouthful of water
                    unbeknownst to the audience.* PROFESSOR *has
                    gotten to his feet and now stands next to*
                    COACH. *Now* PROFESSOR *deliberately spits his
                    mouthful of water into* COACH'S *ear horn.*
                    COACH *then turns and spits a mouthful of water
                    in* MATT'S *face. The illusion is that the water
                    has gone through the ear horn, in* COACH'S
                    mouth and onto MATT'S *face.*)

Professor/ Odysseus	My friends, you have been gracious and hospitable to me Let me tell you how I got here, how my story came to be My horse maneuver worked, allowing us to win the war –
Coach/ Alcinous	(*yelling*) What did you feed it?
Professor/ Odysseus	Feed what?
Coach/ Alcinous	(*yelling*) Your horse. Please tell us some more. How did horse manure keep your glory undiminished?
Professor/ Odysseus	Horse *maneuver,* Helen Keller, now shut up and let me finish. We sailed away like a homesick bunch of lost romantics, Past the Isle of Lesbos for some lovely lesbiantics.
Coach/ Alcinous	(*knowingly nudging* Matt *with his elbow*) I can hear you now!
Professor/ Odysseus	We accidentally sailed off course by many miles and meters, Then finally washed up upon the Land of Lotus-Eaters. The people there were lovely and they greeted us with hugs. Even better, they also gave us mind-expanding drugs. (*Light change. We hear groovy sixties sitar music.* Coach *and* Matt *react as if stoned, then dance offstage.*) It was groovy, fab, and gear, a break from our long mission. But then it took us over and it wiped out our ambition.

> (*He starts to imitate William Shatner.*)
>
> We were acting strangely, poisoned by this
>   magic potion.
> Sulu came out of the closet and Spock finally
>   showed emotion.
> Then I grabbed Uhura and we danced an
>   Arabesque –
>
> (*He slaps his face several times to snap himself out of it.*)
>
> – but I struggled back to normal in a manner
>   Shatner-esque.
> We found a cave we thought would be a
>   protected refuge
>
> (MATT *enters.*)
>
> Until we saw the Cyclops!
>
> (COACH *stomps on as the one-eyed* CYCLOPS. *He has a large single fake eye on the top of his head.*)

COACH/CYCLOPS   Fee fi fo . . .

MATT/SAILOR   Oh my God, that guy is huge!

> (*Using small dolls and high voices,* MATT *and* PROFESSOR *act this out. The dolls are dressed identically to the actors. The dolls knock each other down in their panic.*)

MATT/AUSTIN   (*various*) Run away! Let's get out of here!

PROFESSOR/ODYSSEUS   Greetings, giant person! We are here by accident!

MATT/SAILOR   Can we stay for supper?

COACH/CYCLOPS   Sure!

(COACH *picks up* MATT'S *doll and bites its head, holding it in his mouth.*)

MATT/SAILOR That's not what I meant!

(COACH *shakes the doll and drops it.* COACH *tries to step on the dolls as he says:*)

COACH/CYCLOPS My name is Polyphemus and my father is Poseidon.
If you try to hurt me he will give you quite a hidin'.

PROFESSOR/ODYSSEUS My name is Nobody, good sir.

(MATT *goes "psst!" and holds out a tiny wine bottle.*)

Hey, how 'bout a little wine?

(COACH *takes it from* MATT *and drinks.*)

COACH/CYCLOPS Nobody's a funny name. Is it Greek or Byzantine?

PROFESSOR/ODYSSEUS Nobody's Italian, sir. Please, just keep on drinking

COACH/CYCLOPS Say, this wine's delicious! (*Stiffening.*) Uh-oh. What was I thinking?

(*He falls over unconscious, bouncing on the stage and making the little dolls bounce in reaction.* PROFESSOR *and* MATT *walk the dolls over to the unconscious* CYCLOPS. *They stand on either side of his head, looking into his ears.*)

MATT/SAILOR Hey, Odysseus! I can *see* you!

(*The illusion is that* COACH'S *head is empty.* MATT'S *doll sneezes into* COACH'S *ear and the* PROFESSOR'S *doll flips over, as if the sneeze went into one ear and out the other.*)

Sorry!

(*The dolls start climbing up* COACH, *toward his head. First, they climb over* COACH's *foot . . .*)

PROFESSOR/ODYSSEUS Come on, hurry. Climb up the big hill.

MATT/SAILOR Whee!

(*. . . then over* COACH's *knee . . .*)

PROFESSOR/ODYSSEUS Climb over the medium hill.

MATT/SAILOR Whee!

(*. . . then they trip over* COACH's *crotch.*)

PROFESSOR/ODYSSEUS Uh-oh, tripped over a mole hill.

MATT/SAILOR Eww!

(MATT *hands* PROFESSOR *a pencil, which* PROFESSOR *uses as a spear.*)

PROFESSOR/ODYSSEUS Now's our chance, it's time to put my secret plan to work
This will get us out of here or my name's not Captain Kirk!

MATT/SAILOR Stop it!

PROFESSOR/ODYSSEUS I mean, Odysseus. Hi-yah!

(PROFESSOR *makes the doll stab the pencil into* COACH's *fake eye.*)

COACH/CYCLOPS (*grabbing the pencil*) Ow, I'm being killed!! I must remove this spear!

(The hand holding the pencil has some ripped red fabric hidden in it. COACH dangles the fabric from his hand, creating the illusion of blood pouring out of the eye.)

PROFESSOR/ODYSSEUS: Let's get back to the ship. Come on, let's haul ass outa here!

(The blinded CYCLOPS moves toward the voice, but the doll moves out of the way.)

COACH/CYCLOPS: I swear I'll get you! Come back, Nobody, I will kill you!

PROFESSOR/ODYSSEUS: Ha! My name's Odysseus, not Nobody!

MATT/SAILOR: Shut up, will you?!

(Following the voices, COACH leaps and lands between the two dolls, "launching" them in opposite directions. MATT's doll sails into the audience. If the audience doesn't throw it back immediately, MATT says:)

Little help, please!

(Someone will always toss the doll back onstage. MATT picks it up.)

PROFESSOR/ODYSSEUS: Hey, I wanna try!

(PROFESSOR throws his doll into the audience. He makes a circle with his arms, like a basketball hoop. The audience member will invariably miss. In fact, it's better if they do.)

COACH/CYCLOPS: What the hell. Throw me, throw me!

(He charges to the edge of the stage but stops short. The audience screams as they think that he is going to jump into the crowd. COACH/CYCLOPS the runs off screaming.)

PROFESSOR/ ODYSSEUS
: Quick! He's gone! Let's run away. We really should be going.

MATT/SAILOR
: (*pointing to the audience*) No, I think we should stay here so they can practice throwing!

(MATT *exits.*)

PROFESSOR/ ODYSSEUS
: The ocean made us want to quit and throw in all the towels,
But we landed in Aeaea (*EE-EE-uh.*), The Land Of... Only Vowels.
We met the goddess Circe, and though I love the ladies
I knew she'd show no mercy, so we escaped to Hades!

(*Spooky sounds. Light change.*)

Here in the underworld you have to keep your head,
Because there's no escaping from the mean, ungrateful dead!

(MATT *leaps on dressed as Jerry Garcia with long grey hair and beard, wearing a tie-dyed T-shirt. He has an arrow stuck through his heel. Then* COACH *enters as* KING AGAMEMNON, *with vampire teeth, crown, and cape.*)

Agamemnon! Achilles! Why do you two now appear?

MATT/ACHILLES
: We're dead, you moron.

COACH/ AGAMAMNON
: (*a la Bela Lugosi*) Whaddaya think, we like it here?

MATT/ACHILLES
: I knew the thrill of victory in life, I could not be beat!
But because of my heel I also learned the agony of defeat.

(*The audience groans. The guys glare at them.*)

Well, welcome to Hell!

MATT/COACH (*trying to scare the audience*) Wooo!

PROFESSOR/ODYSSEUS I'm sad you're dead but I'm sure you died with glory!

MATT/ACHILLES Glory?! Are you crazy? Let me tell you a little story.

(MATT *and* COACH *throw* PROFESSOR *to the floor.*)

There's no honor dying for your country, blindly unawares.

COACH/AGAMAMNON The honor comes from making other bastards die for theirs!

MATT/ACHILLES If someone wants your sacrifice, do not volunteer.

BOTH You'd rather be a slave on Earth than emperor down here.

(*The two ghosts leave. Just before they vanish,* COACH *says:*)

COACH/AGAMAMNON Trick or treat! Whee!

PROFESSOR/ODYSSEUS I must get home! I mustn't let these spirits so distract me
And note to self: I mustn't let the Coach or Matt out-act me
(*Rowing over-dramatically.*) We sailed away, facing monsters that were killa.
The worst was that dreaded six-headed monster Scylla!

(MATT *and* COACH *stick their heads and hands into the doorway. They wear headbands with floppy dog ears attached to them and they each have dog puppets on both hands. The effect is six dog heads sticking through the door.*)

MATT/COACH/SCYLLA: Bark! Bark! Bark!

COACH: Sa-right?

MATT: Sa-right!

COACH: So long!

MATT: By-bye!

COACH: (*as he disappears from the doorway*) Whee!

PROFESSOR/ODYSSEUS: We made it past the sirens.

(MATT *and* COACH *re-enter with firemen's helmets and making siren noises. They probably have not had time to remove their Scylla stuff. They circle and exit.*)

Yeah, that was pretty dumb.
Then we stumbled on to the sacred cattle of the sun!
We were warned not to touch the cattle no way, no how
But we really wanted burgers, and this was one mad cow!

(COACH *enters wearing the horse head. Cow horns have been attached lamely to it. He gruffly says, "Moo!", gives the "Up yours" gesture, and exits.*)

At last I'm home. And I can finally have my life back.

(MATT *and* COACH *enter as the suitors. They hold heart shaped boxes of candy.*)

COACH/MATT/ SUITORS: Telemachus, is your mom home?

PROFESSOR/ ODYSSEUS: But I must kill these suitors so I can have my wife back!

(*Big fight scene.* ODYSSEUS *kills all the suitors – all portrayed by* MATT *and* COACH *– with his bow and "arrows." In fact,* ODYSSEUS *grabs a small bow from behind the bookcase, but no arrows. To shoot, he pulls back the string of the bow and then releases it. The suitors hold small half-arrows, out of view of the audience. When they get "shot" by* ODYSSEUS, *they quickly hold the half-arrows up against their torsos. It appears that the arrow is sticking into them, with the quill end sticking out.*)

(ODYSSEUS *shoots* MATT *and then misses* COACH. *Throughout the fight, suitors exit out the doorways after they have been shot.* ODYSSEUS *then shoots at another suitor* (MATT) *who bats the invisible "arrow" away with his sword. The invisible "arrow" flies through the air and hits* COACH *in the head as he enters through the doorway. He screams in pain and exits.*)

(ODYSSEUS *shoots twice more at* MATT, *who with his sword bats the "arrow" away both times. Then* ODYSSEUS *shoots two "arrows" at* MATT. MATT *bats them away, one after the other, and the two arrows hit* COACH *in rapid succession as he enters. He screams in pain and exits.*)

(*Now* ODYSSEUS *takes aim and shoots again at* MATT. MATT *dodges the arrow by bending over backwards in slow motion, a la "The Matrix". The invisible arrow "flies" into the audience. Now back at normal speed,*

PROFESSOR *shoves* MATT *out of the way and goes to retrieve the arrow from under the chair of an audience member.* MATT *exits.* PROFESSOR *ad-libs apologies as he quickly makes his way back to the stage. When he arrives, he lifts up the arrow, revealing it has a large woman's bra hanging from it. He looks shocked, but he mimes putting a phone to his ear and mouths "Call me."*)

Watch this!

(*He "shoots" an arrow toward the stage left wall, then watches it ricochet off the walls three times. After the third ricochet, the single arrow runs through the two suitors – who have entered screaming and with swords drawn – pinning them together. This illusion is created by one of the actors holding a half-arrow against his stomach with a quill showing and the other actor holding a half-arrow against his back with the arrow head showing. They shuffle off stage, still pinned together by the arrow.* PROFESSOR *claps his hands together several times as if to get the dirt off them.*)

Revenge is sweet, but sweeter still's the sight
of my old home.

(MATT/TELEMACHUS *skips on.*)

MATT/ TELEMACHUS	Hi, Dad!
PROFESSOR/ ODYSSEUS	Telemachus! My young son! Look at how you have grown!
MATT/ TELEMACHUS	For twenty years, I've kept mom safe, and our home well-defended.
PROFESSOR/ ODYSSEUS	But by your voice it sounds as though your testes aren't descended.

ALL THE GREAT BOOKS (ABRIDGED)

> And where is she, my delicate young rose,
> Penelope?

(COACH *enters as* PENELOPE, *with ugly wig and skirt. He scratches his crotch.*)

COACH/
PENELOPE

Here I am, Odysseus! Your little chickadee!

PROFESSOR/
ODYSSEUS

> You haven't changed a bit, my love, and my
> poor heart is cheered.
> You both look great. And look, you both have
> a little beard.

(PROFESSOR *feels* COACH'S *stubble.* COACH *slaps the hand away.*)

COACH/
PENELOPE

Knock it off!

MATT/
TELEMACHUS

But gee wiz, dear Father, what are we forgetting?

PROFESSOR/
ODYSSEUS

Let's renew our vows –

COACH/
PENELOPE

And have a great big fat Greek wedding!

(*They step down into their three specials before applause can start.*)

PROFESSOR/
CHORUS

> Thus Odysseus made it home, despite how
> long it took

(COACH *attempts to interrupt, but* PROFESSOR *continues.*)

> Yes, it took awhile, but it's shorter than the
> book.

COACH/CHORUS

> The lesson here is perseverance, please make
> sure you heed it.

MATT/CHORUS The *Idioddity*'s over . . .

ALL . . . and you didn't have to read it.

(They bow. Blackout. The bell rings and lights come back up. COACH *looks at his stopwatch.)*

COACH Alright, class, that bell means it's the end of the first half and time for your midterm examination. Matthew, please distribute the papers.

*(*MATT *has grabbed a stack of midterm papers from the bookshelf and tosses them into the audience. They float down over the crowd.)*

Keep one for yourself, pass the rest along to your neighbors. We also have some very sharp pencils for you to write...

*(*MATT *now runs downstage with a big bunch of yellow pencils that he has grabbed from the bookcase. He acts as if he's going to throw at the audience, but* PROFESSOR *stops him.)*

Matt! No, no! Hand them out or leave them on the edge of the stage. Now, the midterm question you all need to give a written answer to is, "What are the two greatest books ever written and why?"

*(*MATT *has picked up a stack of midterm papers and some pencils from the bookshelf and now places them at the edge of the stage.)*

PROFESSOR We'd like you to write a detailed answer, supported with citations and footnotes. There are extra pencils and midterms right down here. Please sign your name and leave your completed midterms here in a nice neat pile at the edge of the stage.

COACH   We'll begin the second half of the course with what is generally considered the greatest novel of the twentieth century – *Ulysses* by James Joyce. If you have not yet read the book, please do so during this fifteen minute break. Which begins – now!

(COACH *clicks his stopwatch. He blows his whistle and moves his arm in a circle, like a football referee starting the clock. Blackout.*)

End of Act One

ACT TWO

The house lights fade out. The interval music then fades as the stage lights fade to black.

Irish diddly-diddly music begins. A spot rises on COACH *as* STEPHEN DEDALUS, *wearing a flat-cap and wool sweater, and his athletic shorts.*

COACH/STEPHEN (*in an Irish accent*) The name is Stephen Dedalus. I'm on me way to the newspaper to deliver a letter from me boss. But I'm dawdlin' here on the Strand. And I've been feelin' a bit guilty. On her deathbed me mother asked me to pray for her and I refused on principle. I'm an atheist, ya' see. And I'm estranged from me father.

(*Spot fades on* COACH *and rises on* PROFESSOR *as* LEOPOLD BLOOM, *holding a can of Guinness. He wears a cap and somewhat worn suit coat.*)

PROFESSOR/ BLOOM (*in an Irish accent*) I'm Leopold Bloom. I'm in advertisin'. I'm on me way to the newspaper to secure some advertisin' space. Me wife Molly Bloom and I haven't had marital relations in over eleven years, since the death of our infant son shortly after birth.

(*If the audience laughs after "eleven years,"* PROFESSOR *can skip the rest of the line and say, "Think that's funny, do ya?" He drinks from the Guinness and freezes. Spot fades on* PROFESSOR *and rises on* MATT *as* MOLLY BLOOM, *wearing a bad wig and skirt.*)

MATT/MOLLY (*in an American accent*) I'm Molly Bloom, Leopold Bloom's wife. I talk like an American because my Irish accent's crap. I'm about to undertake a concert tour under the management of Blazes Boylan. We're having an affair.

(*He winks as the spot light cross fades to* COACH. *Then* COACH'S *recorded voice comes over the loudspeaker.* COACH's *lips don't move.*)

COACH (*VO*) *Wow! The book* Ulysses *was groundbreaking on so many levels. It's not so much about the physical actions of the characters, but about their interior life, their thoughts and motivations. And I love Joyce's use of inner monologue.*

(*Cross fade to* PROFESSOR, *who speaks out loud as* BLOOM.)

PROFESSOR/ BLOOM It's June sixteenth, nineteen hundred and four. Stephen Dedalus and I are wanderin' around Dublin. I'm a bit of a father figure to Stephen. Though because of my Jewishness, I'm an outsider in me own land.

(*The audience doesn't react the way he expects. He stares at them and his thoughts come over the sound system. Your sound operator will need to be able to pause the recording to ride out laughs at various points in the rest of the scene. Fairly consistent laughs are marked with an asterisk [*].*)

PROFESSOR/ BLOOM (*VO*) *I hate this audience.* Look at all those blank stares. These people have no idea what* Ulysses *is about.*

(*The lights fade up on each person as he speaks, and then dim as they finish.*)

COACH (*VO*) *This audience has no idea what* Ulysses *is about.*

MATT (*VO*) *I have no idea what* Ulysses *is about.**

PROFESSOR (*VO*) *What's everybody laughing at? I hate this audience.*

MATT (*VO*) *I wonder if the audience has figured out that we haven't read any of these books?*

COACH   (*VO*) *Does this costume make me look fat?*

                     (PROFESSOR *and* MATT *shake their heads in the negative, but we hear their actual thoughts which are . . .*)

PROFESSOR   (*VO*) *Yeah.*

MATT   (*VO*) *Of course it does.*

PROFESSOR   (*VO*) *Like the south end of a horse going north . . .*

COACH   (*VO*) *Hey wait a minute! How did you hear my inner monologue?*

PROFESSOR   (*VO*) *Uh oh! I think our thoughts are being broadcast over the sound system.* (*Smiling at the audience.*) *I love this audience!*

MATT   (*VO*) *Hey Coach, I don't have an inner monologue.*

COACH   (*VO*) *Really? Then what do I hear every time you have a thought?*

                     (MATT *looks up, listening. We hear crickets chirp three times.*)

                     Now go ahead and finish up Ulysses.

                     (COACH *and* PROFESSOR *start to exit.* MATT *stands in the centre spotlight.*)

MATT   (*VO*) *What am I supposed to do?*

COACH   (*VO*) *Just do the Molly Bloom speech at the very end of the book. It's her great life affirming, stream of consciousness inner monologue*

MATT   (*VO*) *I can't. I'm telling you, I don't have an inner monologue.*

PROFESSOR (*VO*) *I'll do it. Gimme that.*

(*He takes the wig and puts it on.* COACH *and* MATT *exit.*)

Here goes.

(*We now hear a female Irish voice.*)

MOLLY BLOOM (*VO*) *Then he held me under the Spanish Arch and I thought, why not him as anyone else and then I looked into his eyes and he asked me again yes and wondered if I would yes my . . .*

(PROFESSOR *has slowly become aware that this is not his voice. He looks around discreetly for the source of it, then:*)

PROFESSOR (*VO*) *Wait a minute . . . whose inner monologue is this?*

MOLLY BLOOM (*VO*) *Yours.*

PROFESSOR (*VO*) (*confused*) *Why doesn't it sound like me?*

MOLLY BLOOM (*VO*) *I don't know.*

PROFESSOR (*VO*) (*in a panic*) *Am I schizophrenic?*

MOLLY BLOOM (*VO*) *I don't know!*

(PROFESSOR *mouths "Oh my God," grabs his head with both hands and bends over as if in pain. The female voice draws his attention up again.*)

. . . and he asked again yes and wondered if I would yes my meadow blossom and then I held him in my arms yes and pulled him close to me against my . . .

PROFESSOR (*VO*) *I'm sorry to interrupt, but I must say you have a lovely voice.*

ACT TWO

MOLLY BLOOM   (*VO*) *Thank you. And pulled him close to me...*

PROFESSOR   (*VO*) *What are you wearing?**

MOLLY BLOOM   (*VO*) *Nothing.*

PROFESSOR   (*VO*) *Really?*

MOLLY BLOOM   (*VO*) *I'm an inner monologue!*

PROFESSOR   (*VO*) *Right! Right. I'm sorry. My mistake. Please, continue.*

MOLLY BLOOM   (*VO*) *I held him in my arms yes and pulled him close to me against my...*

PROFESSOR   (*VO*) *I'm sorry to interrupt, again, but this is kind of the big climax to* Ulysses. *Would you mind if I took over my own inner monologue?*

MOLLY BLOOM   (*VO*) *It should be a woman.*

PROFESSOR   (*VO*) *Aw, please? As a favour from one inner monologue to another?*

MOLLY BLOOM   (*VO*) *Okay. Fine.*

PROFESSOR   (*VO*) *Great.*

MOLLY BLOOM   (*VO*) (*sotto voce*) *Stupid eedjit.*

(PROFESSOR *looks up – what did you say? – then moves on.*)

PROFESSOR   (*VO*) *Okay, let's see . . . and then I held him in my arms yes and pulled him close to me against my bosom . . .*

(*He slows down during this, getting a little uncomfortable.*)

You know what? You were right. It should be a woman. Why don't you go ahead and finish this up? (Pause.) Hello?

MOLLY BLOOM *(VO) No. I've had it. Finish the damn thing yourself.*

PROFESSOR *(VO) But you were right, it should be a woman.*

MOLLY BLOOM *(VO) Finish it yourself. Goodbye!*

(We hear footsteps walking away.)

PROFESSOR *(VO) Wait! Come back!*

MOLLY BLOOM *(VO) Good-bye!*

(We hear a door slam. PROFESSOR *is puzzled how a voice can leave rooms and slam doors, but decides to move on.)*

PROFESSOR *(VO) Forget it. Here goes. (Simply.) And then I held him in my arms yes and pulled him close to me against my bosom all perfume and his chest was pounding and yes I told him yes I would yes . . .*

(On the final 'yes', he bows. The lights fade to black. Lights up. MATT *is on stage collecting the midterms from the edge of the stage (where the audience has left them during interval). He hands some to* COACH *and* PROFESSOR.*)*

(Incidentally, there should be twenty-eight books left on stage at the interval. The rest have been carried up to the bookshelf during Act One. If you put one more book on stage during intermission (we suggest a book that actually opens, that you can use for Anna Kareninokova), you will have twenty-nine. Then, when you finish the "one sentence book review" at the end of the show, all the books should have been picked up.)

COACH

All right, that was *Ulysses* by James Joyce. But now it's time to grade your midterms. And I'm sure we got some wonderful answers to our question, "What are the two greatest books ever written and why?"

PROFESSOR

Here's an interesting answer. Steve McDonald . . . ? (*He looks around to see if Steve will identify himself. Feel free to use names here that actually sound like the names of people who might live in your locale. He reads.*) Steve McDonald says, "The greatest book ever written is the dictionary. It contains every word, so in a sense it contains every book ever written." All right, I'll give you that.

MATT

Here's a good one. Susie Epperson writes, (*Reading.*) "*Green Eggs and Ham*, I enjoy the rhyming." I agree! "I do not lie there in the grass/I will not take it up the – "

PROFESSOR/COACH

Matt!

MATT

(*grading the answer*) A.

COACH

Mark Monforti says, "The greatest book ever is *Moby Dick*. Ha, ha, ha. I just made you say, 'Dick.'" Okay, if that's the way it's going to be, that's the way it's going to be!

(*He storms off.*)

PROFESSOR

Coach, come back.

MATT

Aw, let him go, his jock strap's too tight.

PROFESSOR

Wow, listen to this. Robin Selinger – Robin? – says . . . (*Reading.*) "The greatest book ever written is *Pat the Bunny*. This story combines magic realism with a sensual tactile experience sure to provide a *frisson* of pleasure to even the most jaded of readers. The indeterminate gender of the bunny adds to the mystery of this classic tale, and calls into question our assumptions about traditional family values." (*He looks at the class, amazed.*) What are you doing in the remedial class?

(COACH *enters dressed as* AHAB, *wearing a head scarf. He hops on one leg.*)

COACH/AHAB The whale! Have you seen the Great White Whale?

PROFESSOR What are you doing?

COACH/AHAB They want Dick? I'll give 'em Dick!

MATT Hey!

PROFESSOR Coach, we're doing the midterms now. Stop hopping!

COACH/AHAB (*stopping*) Don't give me that! I control men by my sheer force of will. (*He grimaces as though trying to communicate telepathically.*)

PROFESSOR Now what are you doing?

COACH/AHAB I'm controlling you by my sheer force of will! (*He grimaces again.*)

PROFESSOR You look like you're having a poo.

(PROFESSOR *exits.* COACH *stops grimacing.*)

COACH/AHAB I hate it when you ignore my sheer force of will! (*He starts hopping again.*)

MATT Coach, I've got your sheer force of will, but I don't understand why you're hopping.

COACH/AHAB The whale took my leg. I must take his life. I need to board the *Pequod* and head for the open sea. I need the wind at my back, the sea in my face!

Act Two

(PROFESSOR *runs on and tosses a bucket of water in* COACH'S *face.*)

MATT Hey!

COACH What did you do that for?!

PROFESSOR I was adding some realism.

COACH Forget it!

(COACH *storms off.*)

MATT No, you weren't. You threw water in his face.

PROFESSOR I know, did you see the spray!

MATT Why don't you let him do his character?

PROFESSOR I was helping.

MATT That ain't not helping!

PROFESSOR (*beat*) That ain't not English. Apparently I need to explain. (*To the audience.*) In the theatre we call what I just did "yes-anding".

MATT Yeah, well in the real world we call it "censor-shipping"! This is how book banning starts. You were intimidating him.

PROFESSOR Wait – throwing water is intimidation?

MATT Of course.

PROFESSOR Right, I remember when Stalin threw water on the peasants. What the hell are you – ?

MATT Oh cute. You demean what I say by making fun of it. That's a form a censorship. Do you realize they're now banning books like *Diary of Anne Frank* and *Of Mice and Men*?

ALL THE GREAT BOOKS (ABRIDGED) 71

PROFESSOR   Who are?

MATT   Schools across the country, that's who are.

PROFESSOR   That's not true!

MATT   It is true! Students, we need to mount an international campaign to put these books back on the shelves. Are you with me? 'Cause if people . . .

(*The crowd cheers. If they don't,* PROFESSOR *changes the following line to, "First of all, it doesn't sound like anybody's with you. And secondly, the books you're talking about are available everywhere." In any event,* PROFESSOR *interrupts* MATT, *and if the crowd makes noise says:*)

PROFESSOR   Matthew, before you and your friends mount anything you should know the books you're talking about are available everywhere.

MATT   Right, pretty soon they're gonna start banning some really important books, like the manual to my Nintendo Wii.

PROFESSOR   I don't want to know what you are doing manually to your wee. It's a *Brave New World*.

(*He grabs* MATT'S *midterms away from him.*)

MATT   Stop doing that! This is just like when John Lennon said The Beatles were more popular than Jesus. Everybody freaked out and started burning their Beatles records. And now, computer companies are telling you to burn CDs! That's right, "Burn your own CDs! Music is evil!"

PROFESSOR   Matthew! Burning CDs is a good thing!

MATT   Oh-h-h! I knew you'd say something like that! You are just like those religious freaks who are

ACT TWO

	banning *Harry Potter* because it promotes witchcraft? Now you can't find *Harry Potter* books, the movies, or the merchandise anywhere.
PROFESSOR	Sure you can. Matthew, I am just as against book banning as you are.
MATT	Right. You're not getting into my head, Nurse Ratched.
PROFESSOR	(*as* MATT *covers his ears and sings or makes noises or screams*) Books should not be banned. No art should be . . .
	(*They argue strongly.* COACH *enters and blows his whistle.*)
COACH	Look, you two are never going to agree, so we're just moving on to those three great British authors.
PROFESSOR	Thank you!
MATT	Great, I'll get the books together –
	(MATT *starts to cross to the bookshelf, but* COACH *cuts him off.*)
COACH	By the way, Matt, did you ever get to the bottom of the sneezing business?
MATT	Yeah, actually Coach, I have . . .
COACH	Good.
MATT	It's pretty funny, I have a little confession to make . . .
COACH	I am going to kick this guy's ass!
MATT	Really?
COACH	Who is it?

MATT	Him!

(MATT *points to a man in the audience.*)

COACH	Oh, really? A comedian right here in the front . . . (*Or second, or third, or whatever.*) . . . row!

(*As* COACH *makes his way down to the guy,* MATT *and* PROFESSOR *take focus.*)

PROFESSOR	Wait, what happened?
MATT	Oh yeah! "Whenever Coach says Plato, everybody sneeze!" Sorry, man . . .
PROFESSOR	So he's the ringleader?
MATT	No, it was me. C'mere . . .
PROFESSOR	What?
COACH	What's your name? (*The audience member tells him.*) Name of audience member . . . ladies and gentlemen!

(*As the audience applauds,* COACH *asks the audience member to help out and gets his permission. They come onstage as* MATT *and* PROFESSOR *exit.*)

COACH	Well, I don't appreciate your shenanigans. I'm going to have to make an example of you in front of the entire class. I'll let you know when I need you. Right now, we're going to learn about three great British authors, their lives and their work.

(*He now reads the introductions from note cards that he's pulled out of his pocket. There are nine cards, one for each author's introduction, and one for each of the six questions that follow.*)

Our first author is an English woman who never married. Her books deal with middle class people and their daily routine. Her most famous novels are *Sense and Sensibility* and *Pride and Prejudice*. Please bang your hands together for – say it with me now – Jane Austen!

(MATT *enters, wearing a blonde wig and skirt.*)

How are you doing, Jane?

MATT/JANE   No, Coach, how *you* doing?

COACH   Just fine. Author Number Two was a religious zealot until her twenties. She wrote under a man's name so that her work would be taken seriously and her best known books are *Silas Marner* and *Middlemarch*. Give it up for – say it with me now – George Eliot!

(PROFESSOR *enters, wearing a black wig and skirt. He has a blonde curly wig tucked into the back of the skirt so the audience can't see it.*)

PROFESSOR/   Hi, Coach. Hi, Jane.
G ELIOT

COACH   George, (*Audience guy's name*) . . . (*Audience guy's name*), George.

PROFESSOR/   Hi, (*audience member's name*).
G ELIOT

COACH   Author Number Three wrote *Orlando* and *To The Lighthouse*, and was a member of the Bloomsbury Group. After several nervous breakdowns, she drowned herself at age fifty-nine. But there's no reason to be afraid of – say it with me – Virginia Woolf!

(PROFESSOR *holds out the blonde wig to* COACH, *as if* COACH *is supposed to put it on. But* COACH *takes a step back and looks at the audience guy.* PROFESSOR *helps the guy put on the wig.*)

(*presenting*) Virginia Woolf!

PROFESSOR/ G ELIOT
(*presenting*) Peter Frampton! (*Or Roger Daltry or Twisted Sister or Shakira, whichever blond curly rocker your audience will recognize.*)

COACH
Okay, let's learn about these authors. Jane Austen...

MATT/JANE
Yes?

COACH
Critics have noted that there isn't much action in your novels. How would you respond?

MATT/JANE
I think that's a terrible criticism. I've always written from my life experience, and stayed true to myself. And I think my success speaks for itself.

COACH
I think it speaks very loudly.

MATT/JANE
Thank you.

COACH
George Eliot...

PROFESSOR/ G ELIOT
Yes?

COACH
You were one of the first psychological/ sociological novelists. Why were you drawn to this style?

PROFESSOR/ G ELIOT
Interesting. You know, D H Lawrence did say that I was the first to put the action on the inside. I've always felt that a person's interior life and machinations were much more interesting than exterior meanderings.

COACH
I completely agree. Bachelorette Number Three, if I were a banana, how would you peel me?

(If the guy doesn't say anything, COACH goes on to the next line. But as often as not, the audience member will come up with some sort of answer. Sometimes it's a little hard for the audience to hear, so one of the cast members may need to repeat it. In any case, if the volunteer says just about anything in response to the question, it will get a big laugh. The three guys get on their knees, bow down to him, then get up.)

Maybe I should just stick to the cards. Bachelorette Number One, it has been said that *Pride and Prejudice* is a perceptive examination of the relationship between classes in Britain. Do you have a problem with the class system?

MATT/JANE Yes, I do. I don't think the class system works at all.

COACH Really?

MATT/JANE We've been here all night . . . *(Or "day", if it's a matinee.)* . . . and this class hasn't learned a damn thing!

COACH Although I think . . . *(Name of volunteer.)* . . . is learning a little lesson.

PROFESSOR Don't sit in the front row.

(COACH moves on to the next card.)

COACH Bachelorette Number Three, do you have a cold?

(The volunteer will usually say "No." To which COACH replies:)

Then why the hell are you sneezing in my class?!

(If the volunteer says, "Yes," the only difference is that COACH *slightly changes the phrasing to say something like, "Is that why you're sneezing in my class?!")*

MATT/ PROFESSOR
Coach, calm down! Let it go. (*Etc.*) . . .

COACH
Okay, I'll let it go. He's been playing along somewhat manfully. That concludes the questions. The moment of truth is at hand. I am going to go on a dream date with one of these three eligible bachelorettes.

(MATT *and* PROFESSOR *hop up and down and clap in excited anticipation. During* COACH'S *speech,* PROFESSOR *tells* VIRGINIA WOOLF *to join them. He usually does.*)

By your applause, will it be Bachelorette Number One . . . ?

(COACH *gestures to* MATT. *The applause is always weak.* MATT *leaves in disgust.*)

Bachelorette Number Two . . . ?

(COACH *gestures to* PROFESSOR. *Again the applause is weak.* PROFESSOR *goes to the bookcase and takes off his wig and skirt.*)

Or by your applause will it be Bachelorette Number Three?

(*The audience always votes overwhelmingly for Number Three. Catchy game show music plays.* COACH *puts his arm around him and whispers to the volunteer that he's doing great and to hang here for another minute.* MATT *re-enters tossing confetti. He puts Hawaiian leis around the necks of* COACH *and the volunteer. The music fades so* PROFESSOR *can speak over it.*)

PROFESSOR	Congratulations! You lucky kids are going to enjoy a fun-filled romantic weekend getaway trip for two to beautiful . . . (*insert the name of a very ugly nearby town or rundown local kitschy tourist trap or sleazy motel here. This can also be ". . . a romantic candle lit dinner for two at" the least romantic eating establishment in town*)! Let's blow them a kiss goodbye! (*They blow a kiss at the audience.*)
COACH	(*to volunteer*) Look right there. (COACH *points at* MATT, *who takes their picture with a Polaroid camera.* PROFESSOR *gets in the picture, too. They hand the volunteer the photo and then help him offstage.*) (*Audience member's name*), ladies and gentlemen! (COACH *helps him back into the audience, telling him to watch his step.*) One more time . . . (*Name of volunteer.*) . . . everybody!
PROFESSOR	(*as the applause dies*) That's not fair. He doesn't have a script and he's funnier than we are. (COACH *picks up the huge copy of* War and Peace *that's been on the floor since Act One.*)
COACH	The only way to top that is *War and Peace*.
PROFESSOR	(*grabs the book out of* COACH'S *hand*) Woah! No!
MATT	We've already covered *War and Peace*!
COACH	Not to my satisfaction.

PROFESSOR	Coach, we still have all these books left to cover before graduation. (*Picking one up from the floor.*) Let's just do something simple, like Dante's *Divine Comedy*.
COACH	Okay, one thing you need to know about *The Divine Comedy*. Not funny. This genius wrote a comedy and he left out the jokes. It's like *Carrot Top*. (*Or whoever is the least funny comedian that everyone has heard about.*)
	(COACH *tosses the book upstage.*)
MATT	Coach, why don't we cover that other novel by Tolstoy, you know, the one about the sexy Russian tennis player who throws herself under a train?
	(COACH *picks it up from the floor and hands it to* MATT.)
COACH	Anna Kareninakova?
MATT	Yeah!
	(*He opens the book and turns it lengthwise, like a centrefold. Then he carries it upstage and places it on the bookshelf.*)
COACH	Guys, don't be so afraid of *War and Peace*. (*To the audience.*) If you take nothing else away from this course, take this: do not be intimidated by the great authors. They were regular guys. They put their trousers on one leg at a time.
PROFESSOR	What about Emily Brönte?
COACH	She put her dress on one leg at a time.
MATT	Gertrude Stein?
COACH	Not sure.

PROFESSOR   Coach, I have a confession to make. I couldn't finish reading *War and Peace*.

MATT   Me, either.

COACH   (*to* MATT) How far did you get?

MATT   Introduction.

COACH   Well, you're both pathetic. (*Handing* War and Peace *to* MATT.) I finished it and it's fantastic. It's got everything: life and death, love and hate, war and peace. You name it, it's in here.

(MATT *has opened the huge book.* COACH *pulls out the small* War and Peace *study guide tucked inside.* MATT *carries the big* War and Peace *up to the bookshelf.*)

PROFESSOR   Anybody can read the study guide! But I couldn't finish the real book. I'm not man enough.

COACH   Well, Matt is.

MATT   No, I'm not.

PROFESSOR   No, he's not!

COACH   You're not man enough?

(*They argue briefly until* COACH *blasts his whistle.*)

Take a knee, fellas.

(*They kneel. Dramatic music plays.* COACH *paces.*)

Where the hell did that music come from? I know you're scared. You feel like it's the end of regulation and you're down four-nil. Well, look at the bright side. At least you're not a season ticket holder for the Los Angeles Clippers. (*Or your crappy local sports team.*). Tolstoy said that men are controlled by destiny. Well this our destiny, men. We did not choose *War and Peace*. *War and Peace* chose us. Look at these students. There they sit with bright tails and bushy eyes. These are some of the slowest minds in the developed world and they're counting on us. So let's get out there and tackle *War and Peace*. The longest novel in the history of Russia!

ALL   U! S! A! U! S! A! U! S! A! U! S! A! U! S! A!

(*They run offstage. Epic music begins.* MATT *enters, walking very formally, wearing a Russian fur cap and with a large sign rolled up under his arm. He stops and reveals the sign which is written in Russian. This actual Russian text is printed on page 112 of this script. In the original production the sign said, in Russian, "This is actual Russian. Are you impressed?" He then reveals the other side of the sign which reads,* "COACH *is making a very long costume change." He exits.* COACH *enters wearing a military coat and a really bad wig and strikes a pose. The audience laughs. With a hand gesture of encouragement, he gets the audience to applaud him.*)

COACH/ANDREY   Page One. I am Andrey Bolkonsky. Against the background of Napoleon's impending invasion of Russia, I am attending a massive society party in Saint Petersburg, at which we meet all of the major characters of *War and Peace*.

(PROFESSOR *enters.*)

PROFESSOR/PIERRE   Page Five. I am Pierre ... (*Coughing nastily.*) ... Nastykhov. (*He stares down the audience.*)

COACH/ANDREY (*to* PIERRE) Page twenty-two. I am cynical and arrogant, at war with my father's outdated feudal values.

PROFESSOR/PIERRE (*to* ANDREY) Page fifty-five. Despite my youth, I am thoughtful and optimistic – completely at peace with myself.

COACH/ANDREY Wait! I'm at war...

PROFESSOR/PIERRE ... and I'm at peace!

(*They laugh and embrace in the manly Russian style.* MATT *enters as* NATASHA, *stepping between them.*)

MATT/NATASHA Introduction. I am Natasha Rostov – the embodiment of innocent feminine sexuality. Hello, boys!

COACH/ANDREY Will you marry me?

MATT/NATASHA Yes, Andre, of course.

PROFESSOR/PIERRE But I am the fictional embodiment of Tolstoy himself.

MATT/NATASHA It never hurts to sleep with the author.

(NATASHA *shoves* ANDREY *aside and exits with* PIERRE, *arm in arm.*)

COACH/ANDREY Page eighty-seven. As the embodiment of Mother Russia, I join the army to fight at the front, seeking honour and glory.

(*We hear the sounds of battle.* COACH *mimes shooting a rifle.*)

Bang! Bang! Bang! (*He mimes being shot.*) Great bowls of borscht! I'm shot.

(We hear heavenly harps.)

Wait! I'm having . . . *(He lifts his wig off his head with both hands and then puts it back on – as if it briefly floated away from his head.)* . . . an epiphany. And it's hair raising!

(He exits. PROFESSOR shoves MATT on, protesting.)

MATT   But, I don't – page . . . page . . . ?

(MATT obviously doesn't know what's next. COACH sticks his head out.)

COACH   One thirty-five!

(COACH tosses MATT the study guide and exits.)

MATT   Page one thirty-five. Oh! Russian nicknames are explained. The suffix "Ovich" means "son of." Hence, Ivanovich means "son of Ivan." Interesting.

(MATT dashes off as PROFESSOR runs on.)

PROFESSOR/PIERRE   Page one seventy-eight. I decide to assassinate Napoleon, that bitchovich.

(PROFESSOR exits. COACH enters.)

COACH/ANDREY   Page two eighty-five. My father receives word that I have died. *(Beat)* I know the feeling.

(COACH exits. PROFESSOR pulls MATT on. MATT's furiously leafing through the study guide.)

PROFESSOR   Page three oh-four. Natasha Rostov decides she doesn't want to marry Boris!

(PROFESSOR exits.)

ACT TWO

MATT/
NATASHA
(*picking up his cue*) No, I don't want to marry Boris! Wait, who's Boris? Who's Boris?!

(*He exits.* COACH *enters.*)

COACH/ANDREY Page three fifty-four. I'm not really dead, but I return home and scare my wife so badly that *she* dies.

(*Trying to be helpful,* MATT *runs on, screams, throws his study guide in the air and drops dead.* COACH *shakes his head and exits.* MATT *leaps up, totally lost. He flips through the study guide trying to figure out what's next.*)

MATT
Um, 1983. Mikhael Gorbachov spills ketchup on his head!

(MATT *tosses the study guide in the air, then crosses upstage.* COACH *runs on.*)

COACH/ANDREY Page four oh-four. Russia's transition from an agricultural to an industrial society is mirrored by my arrival at the family estate . . .

(MATT's *now standing behind* COACH. *He snatches the wig off* COACH's *head.*)

. . . Bald Hills.

(COACH *exits.* MATT *strokes the toupee.*)

MATT/
NATASHA
(*a la Gollum*) Precious. My precious.

(MATT *exits as* PROFESSOR *runs on.*)

PROFESSOR
Page four seventy-one. My assassination attempt fails. The war continues.

(*We again hear the sounds of battle.* MATT *runs on as* PROFESSOR *exits.*)

MATT
In 1989, the Soviet Union falls.

(MATT *turns to try and pick up the study guide, but* PROFESSOR *runs on fast and knocks* MATT *down.* PROFESSOR *quickly makes sure* MATT'S *okay, then says:*)

PROFESSOR In 2008 (*Or whatever year it is.*) Matthew falls.

MATT Page four seventy-three. Why don't you open your eyes, Professor? I was standing right there!

(MATT *exits.*)

PROFESSOR (*surprised*) Page four eighty-five. At least I know the difference between "invincible" and "invisible".

(MATT *runs back on.*)

MATT Page four ninety-three. Stop censoring me and get off your high horse!

PROFESSOR Oh, you wanna go there? Page four ninety-eight! Hell freezes over when you actually read one of the books we're trying to teach!

MATT Well, I guess that brings us to page five hundred. What do you know? Bite me!

(*He heaves the study guide at* PROFESSOR, *who's caught off-guard.*)

PROFESSOR Wha– How dare you?!

(*Their argument escalates until* COACH *enters and stops them with his whistle.*)

COACH This is a war! Stop fighting!

PROFESSOR Coach, we're wasting time on *War and Peace*. We should be covering all these books. (*He takes off his Russian peasant shirt as he speaks.*) And you know what? Tolstoy was wrong. We do have free will and I'm exercising mine right now!

(*He throws his peasant shirt upstage, and starts to exit, but he stops as he hears* MATT's *next point.*)

MATT
Look, I hate to agree with him, but Professor's right. What is your obsession with *War and Peace?* You know we still have to cover *The Grapes of Wrath!*

PROFESSOR
Yeah, and Sherlock Holmes!

MATT
The Scarlet Letter!

PROFESSOR
The Three Musketeers!

MATT
(*a la Bela Lugosi*) *Dracula!*

PROFESSOR
Dr Jekyll and Mr Hyde!

COACH
Don't you understand? If we finish *War and Peace* we've covered all those books! It has the swordplay of *The Three Musketeers*, the infidelity of *The Scarlet Letter*, the mystery of Sherlock Holmes, and the inhumanity of *The Grapes of Wrath.*

(COACH *crosses toward the bookshelf.* PROFESSOR *follows him.*)

PROFESSOR
But we haven't finished reading *War and Peace,* so how can we go on?

(MATT *kneels and ties his shoe.*)

MATT
(*innocently*) Well, you know what, Tolstoy said it himself. Don't over-think. Be in the moment. Forget reason and strategy, and simply have faith in the human spirit. Live your life instinctively, with a passion for spontaneity.

(PROFESSOR *and* COACH *stare at* MATT, *who suddenly realizes they're looking at him.*)

Apparently somebody didn't read the introduction.

COACH   Page eight hundred and seventy-seven. The climax of *War and Peace*, the battle of Borodino. Bring it in.

(COACH *puts out his hand, calling them over to huddle.* MATT *and* PROFESSOR *put their hands on top of* COACH'S.)

ALL   One, two three – Tolstoy!

(*They push their hands down – a huddle break. The* 1812 Overture *begins.* MATT – *who's still holding* COACH'S *wig – tosses the wig up into the air.* MATT *and* PROFESSOR *exit.* COACH *catches the wig on his head.*)

COACH/ANDREY   Toss me my weapon!

(PROFESSOR *tosses* COACH *the stick horse.* COACH *catches it and holds as if it's a rifle.*)

Stand behind me, men! Napoleon will take no prisoners! There is no such thing as polite war! No magnanimity to the enemy . . .

(MATT *runs on and hits* COACH *with a soccer ball. All the balls are in fact inflatable beach balls shaped like various sports balls.*)

MATT   Attack! Attack!

(MATT *hits* COACH *with a ball and exits.*)

COACH/ANDREY   (*improvising*) The French are firing cannon balls!

(PROFESSOR *runs on from the other wing and hits* COACH *with a ball.*)

COACH	What are you doing?!
PROFESSOR	We're controlled by destiny!

(*He hits* COACH *with another ball and exits.*)

COACH	Stop it!

(MATT *has entered with an entire bag of balls.*)

MATT	We can't! (*Chucking a ball at* COACH.) We have not chosen the balls. The balls have chosen us!

(MATT *fires another ball at* COACH, *then starts throwing balls to the audience.*)

COACH	This isn't in *War and Peace!*

(PROFESSOR *has entered with a whole bag of balls. He throws one at* COACH.)

PROFESSOR	*Au contraire, mon petite fromage!* (*Hitting him with another one.*) You said *everything* is in *War and Peace!*

(PROFESSOR *and* MATT *empty their ball sacks into the front row and encourage the class to chuck the balls at* COACH.)

PROFESSOR/ MATT	(*various*) Attack! Attack! Throw those at Coach!

(*They exit. The audience throws the balls at* COACH *and he dodges/kicks/hits/throws/bats the balls away.*)

COACH	Bring it on! Is that all you got? Whaddaya, play for the _____? (*Local terrible team.*) (*Referring to audience member who has just thrown a ball at him.*) And you, ma'am, have got a lot of balls! (*Trying to get back on track.*) I have abandoned my wife and children

because I do not expect to live out this day.
War is to the death, and I fully expect to die!

(MATT *and* PROFESSOR *run back on dressed as musketeers. They carry long metal foils – in fact,* MATT *carries two. He wears Mickey Mouse ears and large white Mickey Mouse gloves. The audience laughs.* PROFESSOR *notices what* MATT *is wearing.* COACH *drops his stick horse and wig on the stage.* MATT *tries to act dignified but the audience keeps laughing. In frustration, with his silly glove,* MATT *gives the audience the 'V-sign'.*)

COACH/ PROFESSOR: (*various*) Hey! Knock it off!

(MATT *tosses a sword to* COACH.)

COACH: Who the hell are you?

MATT: The Three Mouseketeers!

PROFESSOR: Musketeers, dumb-ass!

MATT: (*with great dignity*) It's pronounced Dumas (*Doo-MAH*).

PROFESSOR: I am D'artagnan!

MATT: And I am Minnie Mouse!

COACH/ PROFESSOR: Stop it!

PROFESSOR: It's all for one!

MATT: And every man for himself! *En garde, monsieur!*

(COACH *duels with* PROFESSOR *while* MATT *cowers.* PROFESSOR *waves his musketeer plume in* COACH's *face, and* COACH *bats it away.*

Finally, they get up close to each other, nose to nose. PROFESSOR rubs COACH's forehead.)

PROFESSOR: Look! I can see myself!

COACH: Really?

(COACH *head butts* PROFESSOR, *who runs off holding his head.* MATT *tries to exit but* COACH *stops him.*)

What part of France are you from?

MATT: Disneyland Paris!

(*There is a brief bit of swordplay, with* MATT *ending up near the doorway.* COACH *throws him through one door and* PROFESSOR *flies on through the other, dressed as* SHERLOCK HOLMES.)

PROFESSOR/SHERLOCK: Quickly, Watson! The game's afoot!

COACH: (*confused*) What the hell is going on?

(*They start dueling.*)

PROFESSOR/SHERLOCK: Elementary, my dear Coach!

(SHERLOCK *parries* COACH's *sword attack with his pipe. The pipe breaks to* SHERLOCK's *chagrin and* COACH's *delight.*)

Bollocks.

(*They continue fighting.*)

Your assertion is that *War and Peace* contains the elements of all the great books. Do you deny it?!

COACH: I do not!

PROFESSOR/ SHERLOCK
Ah-ha! Then you'll be overjoyed when Matthew and I illustrate the rest of *War and Peace* with our favorite characters from fiction!

(MATT *comes on dressed as Dracula, with false teeth he can barely speak through.*)

MATT/DRACULA I am Dracula!

(MATT *"accidentally" spits out his fake teeth and they land onstage.*)

MATT/DRACULA I'm traveling to London, vere I vill . . .

(PROFESSOR *howls like a wolf.*)

Oh, no! It's *Beowulf*!

(*He exits.*)

PROFESSOR/ SHERLOCK
No, Watson. It's the *Hound of the Baskervilles*!

(MATT *runs on wearing a dog nose and howls again.* COACH *exits in disgust.* MATT *follows him. The lights jump to the Walden special, with the previous Walden music. The* PROFESSOR *sits there, fishing like the first two Waldens. The scary shark music is heard over the Walden music.* PROFESSOR'S *pole jerks to the right, then to the left. He's then pulled sharply offstage, screaming.* COACH *and* MATT *enter wearing long ZZ Top-type beards.*)

COACH/MATT The Brothers Karamozov!

(*They briefly juggle bean bags, finish flashily, ta-da and exit.* PROFESSOR *runs on as* DR HENRY JEKYLL, *carrying an Ehrlenmeyer flask full of blue liquid.*)

PROFESSOR/ DR JEKYLL
The long Russian War is over. Napoleon did surrender. What a marvelous party. Pleasure to

meet you. I am Dr Henry Jekyll! (*He drinks out of the Ehrlenmeyer flask.*) Hmm, naughty! (*Suddenly* MR HYDE.) But nice! Join me, friends!

(MATT *runs through as the* HUNCHBACK OF NOTRE DAME, *ringing a hand bell.*)

MATT/ HUNCHBACK   Sanctuary! Sanctuary!

(MATT *exits.*)

PROFESSOR/ MR HYDE   Ring the bell! Sound the alarm!

(COACH *lumbers through wearing a rubber* FRANKENSTEIN *mask. The face is cut out, so we see* COACH's *face but with the monster's flat head.*)

COACH/ FRANKENSTEIN   Uhh! Uhh!

PROFESSOR/ MR HYDE   Go ravage Madeline Kahn! I have found a way to unleash man's dark side! Nothing can stop me now!

(COACH *has exited.* MATT *enters wearing a Wonder Woman-type bustier with a large "T" on it. He confronts* MR HYDE.)

MATT/TESS   Not so fast, monster. I am Tess! Tess of the D'Urbervilles!

(COACH *re-enters as* HESTER PRYNNE, *wearing a bonnet and an apron with the scarlet "A" on his chest.*)

COACH/HESTER   Leave us alone! We shall not be shamed!

(COACH *curtsies.* PROFESSOR *looks at the letters on their chests.*)

PROFESSOR/ MR HYDE	Oh, no! They've discovered my weakness! "T" and "A"!

(COACH *chases* PROFESSOR *off.*)

MATT/TESS	I am off! (*A la Buzz Lightyear.*) To the lighthouse, and beyond!

(MATT *exits.* PROFESSOR *hops in on one leg as a pirate.*)

PROFESSOR/LONG JOHN SILVER	Argh! Avast there, mateys. I need to feel the wind at me back, the sea in me face!

(COACH *runs on as* AHAB *and throws a bucket of water on* PROFESSOR. *Then he picks up his stick horse and begins to hop on one leg, too.*)

COACH/AHAB	I'm just trying to add a little realism! *I'm* Captain Ahab! Who do you think you are, ya lily-livered sea monkey?
PROFESSOR/LONG JOHN SILVER	I'm not Captain Ahab! I'm Long John Silver, ya sewage drinkin' bilge rat!
COACH/AHAB	*War and Peace* ain't big enough for two peg-legged caricatures!
PROFESSOR/LONG JOHN SILVER	Oh, yeah? What's a pirate's favorite letter?
COACH/AHAB	Arrr!

(*They have a short sword fight,* PROFESSOR *with a plastic sword and* COACH *using his stick horse. As they fight they say in unison:*)

BOTH	Oh! Aye! See! You! Pee!
COACH	Wait a second! I'm putting my foot down!

(*He does. Without* COACH *being aware of it,* PROFESSOR *charges and impales himself on the stick horse. COACH pulls it out and PROFESSOR exits.)*

I've gotten off-track. I've got to finish *War and Peace* if it's the last thing I do!

(COACH *picks up his toupee off the floor and slaps it on his head. He uses the stick horse as if it were a gun.)*

On page one thousand, Tolstoy condemns the abuse of the lower classes!

(MATT *enters wearing a flat cap and holding a hobo stick.)*

MATT/
TOM JOAD   Whenever there's a cop beating up a guy, I'll be there.

COACH   We are not doing *Grapes of Wrath!*

(COACH *clobbers* MATT *with the stick horse.)*

MATT/
TOM JOAD   Reform the peasantry!

(COACH *hits him again.* MATT *runs off.)*

COACH   Page two thousand and two. Spirituality keeps men from becoming animals.

(PROFESSOR *runs on wearing a pig nose.)*

PROFESSOR   Two legs bad! Two legs bad!

COACH   *Animals!* Not *Animal Farm!*

(COACH *hits* PROFESSOR's *pig nose, knocking it to the floor.* PROFESSOR *runs off as* MATT *runs on in an ape mask. He makes ape noises.)*

No *Origin of Species!*

>   (COACH *punches* MATT, *who exits.* PROFESSOR
>   *returns blowing a conch shell.*)
>
>   Or *Lord of the Flies!*
>
>   (*He sends* PROFESSOR *off by elbowing him in the
>   conch.* MATT *runs on wearing bobbling
>   antennae on his head.*)

MATT   Look, I'm a cockroach! I'm a cockroach! Ha, ha, ha, ha!

>   (COACH *pushes* MATT *to the ground and steps
>   on his bottom, squishing him.* MATT *makes
>   squealing screaming sounds, then lays still.*)

COACH   No Kafka!

>   (MATT *gets up and runs off.*)

          Page three thousand three hundred and thirty-three. Human behavior is irrational. It will always be a mystery!

>   (PROFESSOR *returns as* SHERLOCK HOLMES.)

PROFESSOR/   Wrong again, Inspector Lestrade!
SHERLOCK

>   (COACH *tosses his wig at the* PROFESSOR. *The
>   toupee "attacks"* PROFESSOR'S *throat. He runs
>   off, screaming.*)

COACH   Page ten thousand two hundred and sixteen. The Russian bourgeoise fear that by empowering the lower classes, they will rise up like monsters and kill their former masters.

>   (MATT *returns, dressed and acting like*
>   FRANKENSTEIN.)

          What are you doing?

>   (MATT *tosses the headpiece to the floor.*)

MATT (*pouting as he exits*) You said, "Monsters."

COACH Page twenty-two thousand eight hundred and eleven. *War and Peace* is both the story of a nation and the story of individuals, like a combination of *The Aeneid* and *The Iliad*.

(MATT *runs on as* ACHILLES *in armour and holding a spear, but also with a bandage-wrapped head and dark glasses like The Invisible Man.*)

MATT/ACHILLES I'm Achilles and I am invisible!

(*He stabs* COACH *with his spear.* PROFESSOR *returns as* ODYSSEUS *and does his William Shatner impression.*)

PROFESSOR/ODYSSEUS Beam me up, Scotty. This story sucks!

(*He stabs* COACH *with his sword.*)

COACH We're not doing Ralph Ellison, HG Wells, or William Shatner!

(COACH *grabs* MATT *by the collar and throws him at* PROFESSOR. *They run each other through with their weapons and collapse to the floor.*)

MATT/ACHILLES (*as he dies*) How did he see me . . . ?

PROFESSOR/ODYSSEUS I'm dead, Jim!

(*He dies.* COACH *struggles, dying.*)

COACH Finally, page one million nine hundred and seventy-six thousand two hundred and twenty-five, second paragraph, two-thirds of the way down the page. On his death bed, Andrey comes to understand that life and death, love and hate, war and peace are not opposites.

They are unities. An idea first expressed by
that great Greek philosopher, Plato!

(*The class sneezes.* COACH *falls dead.
Blackout.*)

(*The school bell rings. Lights up.* COACH
clicks off his stopwatch then high fives MATT
and the PROFESSOR. COACH *applauds the class
while* PROFESSOR *bows grandly.*)

PROFESSOR   Thank you, ladies and gentlemen. Thank you
            so much.

            (*But* MATT *stops them.*)

MATT   Wait a minute, we aren't finished. I know you
            all want to get out of here, but we still have all
            these books left to cover.

PROFESSOR   Woah, no!

COACH   Weren't you listening? We did *War and Peace*.
            We're finished.

MATT   Give us about twenty-five more minutes . . .

            (MATT *runs off excitedly.*)

PROFESSOR   Pay no attention to *The Idiot* . . . or other
            books by Dostoevsky. I just want to thank you
            all for coming and let you know that –

            (*But* MATT *returns wearing a high pointed
            wizard's hat and long beard.*)

MATT/GANDALF Join me hobbits! Or you shall not pass!

            (PROFESSOR *and* COACH *just stare.*)

MATT   Come on! Coach, they need to graduate! We
            haven't even done a review.

COACH   We can't. We're out of time.

MATT	Okay, give me two minutes. I can encapsulate each of these great books in a single sentence.
PROFESSOR	No you can't!
MATT	Try me.
	(MATT *takes off his Hawaiian shirt and throws it to the floor.* COACH *clicks his stopwatch to start it.*)
PROFESSOR	Okay. Um . . . *The Origin of Species*.
MATT	We came from apes!
	(PROFESSOR *and* COACH *react, surprised.*)
COACH	*Interpretation of Dreams*.
MATT	I love my mother.
COACH	That's it?
MATT	No, I *really* love my mother.
	(PROFESSOR *grabs a book from the floor.*)
PROFESSOR	Okay, the *Tao*.
MATT	It's the stock exchange in America, but I don't . . .
PROFESSOR	No, not the Dow Jones Industrial Average, the *Tao Te Ching!*
	(*He tosses the book to* MATT.)
MATT	Oh, the *Tao*. Desire nothing.
COACH	*Walden*.
MATT	Simplify your life.

PROFESSOR	*Thus Spake Zarathustra.*
MATT	God is dead.
COACH	*1984.*
MATT	Don't trust the government.
PROFESSOR	*Animal Farm.*
MATT	Don't trust the pigs.
COACH	*The Feminine Mystique.*
MATT	Don't trust – the pigs.

(PROFESSOR *and* COACH *now begin to pick up books from the floor and toss them to* MATT *as they say the title. They don't toss books that have already been picked up and placed on the up-centre bookshelf during the course of the show. They also don't toss books when they say movie titles. By the time the scene is finished, there should be no more books left on the floor.*)

PROFESSOR	(*tossing a book*) *Silent Spring.*
MATT	Don't trust big business.
COACH	(*tossing a book*) *Canterbury Tales.*
MATT	Don't take a long trip with people who like to tell long boring stories. (*He catches each book and stacks them in his arms.*)
PROFESSOR	(*tossing a book*) *Alice in Wonderland.*
MATT	Don't do drugs.
COACH	(*tossing a book*) *On the Road.*
MATT	Do drugs.

PROFESSOR	(*tossing a book*) *Frankenstein.*
MATT	Don't mess with nature.
COACH	*The Odyssey.*
MATT	Don't write a book in Greek that nobody can understand.
PROFESSOR	(*tossing a book*) *Ulysses.*
MATT	Don't write a book in English that nobody can understand.
COACH	(*tossing a book*) *Heart of Darkness.*
MATT	He dies in the end.
PROFESSOR	*Camille.*
MATT	She dies at the end.
COACH	*Sunset Boulevard.*
MATT	Dies at the beginning.
PROFESSOR	*The Bible.*
MATT	Comes back to life at the end!
COACH	(*tossing a book*) *The Great Gatsby.*
MATT	Rich people are screwed up.
PROFESSOR	(*tossing a book*) *Das Capital.*
MATT	The workers are screwed.
COACH	*Oliver Twist.*
MATT	The workers are screwed.
PROFESSOR	(*tossing a book*) *To Kill A Mockingbird.*

MATT	The mockingbirds are screwed!
COACH	(*tossing a book*) *Picture of Dorian Gray*.
MATT	Don't be so obsessed with youth.
PROFESSOR	(*tossing a book*) *Moby Dick*.
MATT	Don't be so obsessed with the whale.
COACH	*Don Quixote*.
MATT	Sanity is overrated.
PROFESSOR	(*tossing a book*) *One Flew Over the Cuckoo's Nest*.
MATT	Sanity is overrated.
COACH	(*tossing a book*) *Harry Potter*.
MATT	Just overrated.
	(*Instead of stacking* Harry Potter *on top of all the books in his arms, he tosses it upstage over his shoulder.*)
PROFESSOR	(*tossing a book*) *For Whom The Bell Tolls*.
MATT	Don't write long sentences.
COACH	(*Tossing* MATT *the* War and Peace *study guide*) *War and Peace*.
MATT	Don't write long books.
PROFESSOR	*Star Wars*.
MATT	Not a book, but Darth Vader is his father.
COACH	*Citizen Kane*.
MATT	Not a book, but Rosebud is his sledge.

PROFESSOR	(*tossing a book*) *Cain and Abel* by Jeffrey Archer. (*This book is well-known in Britain. Feel free to substitute in a best seller of questionable merit that is known in your locale. In America, we use* Dianetics.)
MATT	Not a good book, but people will buy anything.
COACH	(*tossing a book*) *Remembrance of Things Past.*
MATT	I like cookies.
PROFESSOR	(*tossing a book*) *Tom Jones.*
MATT	What's new, pussycat?
COACH	(*tossing a book*) *Beowulf.*
MATT	Don't make us read this crap.
PROFESSOR	(*tossing a book*) *Lolita.*
MATT	Don't be such a pervert.
COACH	(*tossing a book*) *The Fountainhead.*
MATT	Don't rely on anybody else.
PROFESSOR	(*tossing a book*) *Death in Venice.*
MATT	I like that boy, but now I'm dead!
COACH	(*tossing a book*) *Crime and Punishment.*
MATT	I killed that guy, but now I'm dead!
PROFESSOR	(*tossing a book*) *Satanic Verses.*
MATT	I wrote that book, they want me dead!
COACH	(*tossing a book*) *Bridges of Madison County.* (*Again, feel free to substitute the title of a well-known but badly considered book from your locale.*)
MATT	Don't write this crap!!

PROFESSOR	(*tossing the last book*) Gone With The Wind!
MATT	Frankly, my dear . . .
ALL	. . . I don't give a damn!
MATT	Finished!

(MATT *places* Gone With The Wind *atop the huge stack of books in his arms and throws the entire pile up into the air. The school bell rings.* COACH, PROFESSOR *and* MATT *high five each other.* COACH *and* PROFESSOR *point to* MATT *and applaud him. Finally the crowd quiets and* COACH *picks up the fake vampire teeth that fell out of* MATT'S *mouth as Dracula.*)

COACH   And we almost left out *White Fang* by Jack London. (*He casually tosses the teeth over his shoulder.*) Well, we didn't tell you this at the beginning because we knew you wouldn't do the work, but this has been a pass/fail course. Please distribute the diplomas. Congratulations, you all graduate!

(MATT *and* PROFESSOR *each toss a stack of diplomas over the audience. Graduation music begins to play.*)

Thanks for coming. I'm . . . (*Actual name of actor.*)!

PROFESSOR   I'm . . . (*Actual name of actor.*)!

MATT   I'm . . . (*Actual name of actor.*)!

ALL   And this was ALL THE GREAT BOOKS – abridged! Good night!

(*They bow, then high five and run up the aisle and out of the theatre. The end.*)

PROFESSOR'S POEM MEDLEY – ANNOTATED

For scholarly completists (you know who you are) here are the poets and poems referenced by the Professor in his Poem Medley.

There once was a man from Nantucket[1]
Whose string was so long he could pluck it[2]
He shot an arrow in the air
It fell to earth[3], there's no there there[4]
And in the depths of his despair cried, "Fie[5]
On the person who put me here
In the Ballad of Reading Gaol
Where each man kills the thing he loves
And loves the thing he nails.[6]"

Oh . . . Captain! My Captain![7]
We go down to the sea in ships[8]
The rhyming ancient mariner[9] stormed the beach
"Beware the Jabberwock, my son[10]
That dares to part his hair behind[11]
And in Xanadu did Kubla Khan[12] dare to eat a –
Peach[13], bananas, cucumbers . . .

Lettuce go, then, you and I
When evening is spread out amongst the sky[14]
Skylight burning bright[15]
First star I see tonight
Rage rage against the dying of the light
Do not go gentle into Gladys Knight[16]
Two roads diverged in a wood today[17]
How do I love thee? Let me count the way[18]
And I think that I shall never see a poem as lovely as
                                                           Doris Day[19]
Into the valley of the dolls rode the six hundred[20]
On the eighteenth of April in seventy-five[21]
Seventy-six trombones led the big parade[22]
And I was stayin' alive, staying' alive[23]

O body swayed to music, O brightening glance
How can we know the dancer from the dance?[24]
I know why the caged bird sings the body electric[25]
And I'm a maniac
A maniac on the floor[26]
These were my North, my South,
My East, my West,
My noonday lunch, my brekky-fest.[27]
My thoughts are ugly dark and deep[28]
I'd like to choke that little creep
But I cannot for t'would be a sin.
But when your memory's betrayed you
If you don't curse the god that made you
You're a better man than I am . . .
Rin Tin Tin.[29]

POETS/AUTHORS QUOTED (in order of appearance)

Henry Wadsworth Longfellow
Gertrude Stein
Oscar Wilde
Walt Whitman
Samuel Taylor Coleridge
Lewis Carroll
T.S. Eliot
William Blake
Dylan Thomas
Robert Frost
Elizabeth Barrett Browning
Joyce Kilmer
Jacqueline Susann
Alfred, Lord Tennyson
Meredith Willson
The Bee Gees
William Butler Yeats
Maya Angelou
Dennis Matkosky and Michael Sembello
W.H. Auden
Rudyard Kipling

(Footnotes)

[1] Perhaps the most famous line in the entire poem. As far as we can discover, it was penned by the most prolific writer who ever lived – Anonymous.

[2] We first heard this uttered by Edward Herrmann on a classic episode of "St Elsewhere", probably written by Tom Fontana. As to its real authorship, a Google search turns up two sites dedicated to Edna St Vincent Millay and one dedicated to Nathaniel Hawthorne, both of whom apparently loved to use the words 'string', 'long', and 'pluck', but never (as far as we can tell) in the precise order used here. So what the hell – let's say Edna St Vincent Millay.

[3] Here we go, the first genuine line of poetry written by an identifiable person. In "The Arrow and the Song", Henry Wadsworth Longfellow wrote 'I shot an arrow into the air/It fell to earth, I knew not where . . ."

[4] Gertrude Stein coined this phrase. She was referring (inaccurately, we can attest) to Oakland, California.

[5] Desperately improvised by Professor to curse using a different 'F' word.

[6] Oscar Wilde wrote his famous poem "The Ballad of Reading Gaol" while incarcerated on obscenity charges. One stanza reads, 'Yet each man kills the thing he loves,/By each let this be heard,/Some do it with a bitter look,/Some with a flattering word,/The coward does it with a kiss,/The brave man with a sword.'

[7] Walt Whitman's 'O Captain! My Captain!', written upon hearing of the Assassination of President Abraham Lincoln.

[8] The Professor knows this is a famous poetic phrase, but if he had a gun to his head he couldn't tell you that it's from the 107th Psalm ('They that go down to sea in ships, that do business in great waters: These see the works of the Lord, and his wonders in the deep').

[9] Samuel Taylor Coleridge wrote "The Rime of Ancient Mariner." According to Merriam-Webster's Online Collegiate Dictionary, 'rime' is "an accumulation of granular ice tufts on the windward sides of exposed objects that's formed from supercooled fog or cloud and built out directly against the

wind." The Professor, of course, thinks 'rime' means "words that sound alike."

[10] Lewis Carroll's famous poem "The Jabberwocky" is from his second Alice book *Through The Looking Glass*.

[11] In "The Love Song of J Alfred Prufrock," TS Eliot describes the timid title character as someone who 'dares to part his hair behind'.

[12] This is the opening line of Coleridge's poem "Kubla Khan".

[13] This is TS Eliot again, describing Prufrock's questioning himself: 'Do I dare to eat a peach?' (See footnote 11.)

[14] More Eliot, more "Prufrock": this is a paraphrase of the opening two lines of "The Love Song of J Alfred Prufrock" ('Let us go then, you and I,/When the evening is spread out amongst the sky'). The Professor stumbles onto it because he picks up part of a grocery list and thinks "lettuce" is (are) the first word(s) of the poem.

[15] The Professor is now confusing William Blake's "The Tiger" ('Tiger! Tiger! burning bright') with nursery rhymes.

[16] Now he's confusing Dylan Thomas's "Do Not Go Gentle Into That Dark Night" with the lead singer of "Midnight Train To Georgia." (Interestingly, for some reason, 'rage rage against the dying of the light,' from the same poem, is quoted exactly. This is almost certainly a mistake.)

[17] A paraphrase of the opening line of Robert Frost's poem "The Road Not Taken": 'Two roads diverged in a yellow wood.'

[18] Another paraphrase, this time of Elizabeth Barrett Browning's "How Do I Love Thee?"

[19] The opening stanza of Joyce Kilmer's "Trees" ('I think that I shall never see a poem as lovely as a tree') is mistakenly used to invoke the majesty of kitschy 50s goddess Doris Day. Whether this reveals the Professor's desperation to rhyme, or accidentally outs his fondness for camp remains unclear.

[20] Those who believe the Professor's tendency towards camp rises dangerously close to the surface get more evidence here, when he unknowingly references Jacqueline Susann's camp classic "Valley of the Dolls" while attempting to quote Alfred, Lord Tennyson's "The Charge of the Light Brigade"('Into the valley of Death/Rode the six hundred').

[21] This is the third line of the first stanza of Henry Wadsworth Longfellow's "Paul Revere's Ride."

[22] Now hopelessly confused, the Professor is clinging to whatever bits of famous rhymes he can pull out of the air. This line, inspired by the last words of the previous line, is of course from Meredith Willson's *The Music Man*.

[23] The Professor relies on The Brothers Gibb to get him over this rhyming hump.

[24] A last-ditch attempt at an authentically scholarly poem, these are the last two lines of William Butler Yeats's appropriately titled "Among School Children".

[25] In the home stretch now, Professor muddles Maya Angelou's classic volume of autobiography "I Know Why The Caged Bird Sings" with Walt Whitman's "Leaves of Grass", although it's more likely the Professor knows "sing the body electric" as that song from the movie *Fame*.

[26] More evidence of the Professor's fabulously detailed knowledge of 80's movie musicals. Jennifer Beals danced famously to this song in *Flashdance*. It was written by Dennis Matkosky and Michael Sembello.

[27] Professor calls into service here "Funeral Blues," W H Auden's marvelous statement of grief which reads in part, "He was my North, my South, my East and West / My working week and my Sunday rest . . ." Professor knows this poem well, not because he's a huge fan of Auden, but because the poem was featured in *Four Weddings and a Funeral,* which Professor's seen, like, 187 times.

[28] This is Professor's hopefully unconscious paraphrase of Robert Frost's "Stopping by Woods on a Snowy Evening", which in reality goes, "The woods are lovely dark and deep / But I have promises to keep / And miles to go before I sleep."

[29] In his final moments, Professor rises to his own emotional semi-heights by incorporating the meter and rhyme-scheme (but not, unfortunately, the name or its pronunciation, which for the life of him he can't remember) of the last lines of Rudyard Kipling's condescending ode to his "blackfaced" water boy "Gunga Din", which closes thus: "Though I've belted you and flayed you / By the livin' Gawd that made you / You're a better man than I am / Gunga Din!"

The Syllabus

The eighy-seven books that this show claims to cover. Actual Great Books may vary.

(This maybe be used as a program insert.)

1984
The Aeneid
Alice in Wonderland
Animal Farm
Anna Karenina
Autobiography of Alice B Toklas
Beowulf
Brave New World
Bridges of Madison County
The Brothers Karamazov
The Canterbury Tales
A Christmas Carol
The Count of Monte Cristo
Crime and Punishment
Das Capital
David Copperfield
Death in Venice
Dianetics
Diary of Anne Frank
The Divine Comedy
Don Quixote
Dr Jekyll and Mr. Hyde
Dracula
The Feminine Mystique
For Whom The Bell Tolls
The Fountainhead
Frankenstein

Gone With The Wind
The Grapes of Wrath
Great Expectations
The Great Gatsby
Green Eggs and Ham
Harry Potter & the Philosopher's Stone
Heart of Darkness
Hound of the Baskervilles
Huckleberry Finn
Hunchback of Notre Dame
I Know Why The Caged Bird Sings
The Idiot
The Iliad
Interpretation of Dreams
The Invisible Man
Jaws
Leaves of Grass
Little Women
Lolita
Lord of the Flies
Metamorphosis
Middlemarch
Moby Dick
The Odyssey
Of Mice and Men
Oliver Twist
On The Road
One Flew Over The Cuckoo's Nest
The Origin of Species
Orlando
The Picture of Dorian Gray
Plato's Republic
Pride and Prejudice
Remembrance of Things Past
Samuel Johnson's Dictionary

The Satanic Verses
The Scarlet Letter
Sense and Sensibility
Silas Marner
Silent Spring
Sons and Lovers
The Story of Genji
A Tale of Two Cities
Tao Te Ching
TekWar
Tess of the D'Urbervilles
The Three Musketeers
Thus Spake Zarathustra
To Kill A Mockingbird
Tom Jones
To The Lighthouse
Treasure Island
Ulysses
Valley of the Dolls
Walden
War and Peace
White Fang
The Wizard of Oz
Wuthering Heights

Here is the Russian phrase for the sign that is referred to at the beginning of the *War and Peace* section on Page 81:

"Это - фактический русский язык. Вы впечатлены?"